19,86

A

gift from

Twice Told Tales, Ltd.

THE RISE AND OF THE FALL SOVIET UNION

BY MICHAEL KORT

FRANKLIN WATTS
New York | Chicago | London | Toronto | Sydney

FOR
JUDY

Library of Congress Cataloging-in-Publication Data

Kort, Michael, 1944–
The rise and fall of the Soviet Union / by Michael Kort.
p.   cm.
Includes bibliographical references and index.
Summary: A history of the Soviet Union which begins with the conditions leading up to the revolution of 1917 and concludes with the collapse of the Soviet Union in 1991.
ISBN 0-531-11040-0
1. Soviet Union—History.   [1. Soviet Union—History.]
I. Title.
Dk266.K6376   1992
947—dc20   92-23226
CIP   AC

CONTENTS

PREFACE

The failed coup d'etat against Mikhail Gorbachev brought an end to the Soviet Union, the country that is the subject of this book. As these lines are being written in January 1992, a new entity, the Commonwealth of Independent States, has replaced the defunct Soviet Union. But the Commonwealth has replaced the old Soviet Union only to the extent that it occupies most of the territory of the former Soviet Union. The Soviet Union was a highly centralized state; the Commonwealth of Independent States is exactly what the name implies, a loose association of largely independent nations. Both its shape and its future, if it has one at all, remain a mystery yet to unfold. By the time my readers read this book they will know the answers to at least a few of the questions this author can only guess at today. What I hope I can provide for them is an understanding of how the Soviet Union came to be, why Mikhail Gorbachev failed to save the Soviet system, and how the people of this vast country have endured during its troubled history.

⟨1⟩ INTRODUCTION

On March 11, 1985, the Communist party of the Soviet Union chose a new general secretary. The new man in that powerful post was a fifty-four-year-old career politician named Mikhail Gorbachev. Since the Soviet Union was controlled by the Communist party, Gorbachev's selection as its leader meant that he also became the leader of the Soviet Union.

Gorbachev's rise to power came at a difficult time in the history of the country that before 1917 was known as Russia and whose formal name from 1922 to 1991 was the Union of Soviet Socialist Republics. Although in 1985 it was one of the world's two military nuclear superpowers, along with the United States, the Soviet Union was a country in trouble. For most of the 1970s and first half of the 1980s, it seemed unable to cope with its serious domestic problems. Its economy was in a shambles. There was growing tension between the country's many different nationalities and ethnic groups. Cynicism and frustration were widespread and increasing, especially among the country's youth. Serious social problems like alcoholism were affecting the health of millions of Soviet citizens, and the country's life expectancy had actually begun to decline. Corruption in all areas of life was so extensive that it was being accepted as normal.

In addition, despite the Soviet Union's undeniable military power, by the early 1980s its relations with many nations, particularly the United States, were extremely tense. The Soviet Union remained locked in an arms race with the United States that at best was terribly expensive and at worst could lead to the catastrophe of nuclear war. Perhaps most demoralizing, throughout the 1970s and early 1980s the Soviet Union's political leaders not only failed to address these problems, but often appeared not even to recognize that many of them existed.

In a democratic society, citizens at least have the opportunity to remove their leaders if they fail to provide reasonable solutions to urgent problems. This opportunity did not exist in the Soviet Union in 1985, nor had it ever existed there. The Soviet Union was not a democracy, but rather a type of dictatorship known as a totalitarian society. In a democracy, people control their government through free elections, and any number of political parties compete in those elections for the right to govern. In a totalitarian society it is the government that controls the people. The government is controlled by one political party—the only party permitted to exist—which has the real power in the society. Inside that party, decisions are made either by a single dictator, or by a small group of people at the very top.

Elections, if they take place at all, are simply for show and have no effect on those in power. No institutions are allowed to operate independently of the totalitarian party/state, whether they are factories, farms, universities, youth organizations, trade unions, or even sports clubs. The party/state also controls all sources of information, from newspapers and publishing houses to television and radio. In fact, because it controls so many aspects of the people's lives, a totalitarian party/state may be considered a kind of super dictatorship.

The Communist party, the key institution in the Soviet party/state, seized control of Russia in 1917. Although the party exercised dictatorial control over the country from the start, a fullblown totalitarian society did not develop until the 1930s, under the cruel and violent dictatorship of Joseph Stalin, the party's leader at the time. After Stalin died in 1953, his successors ended many of his most brutal policies and did a great deal to improve the lives of the Soviet people. The party/state's control over the people's lives lessened in some important ways. It became easier for workers to choose their jobs and places of residence, for artists and writers to express at least some of their genuine feelings, and for people to get a little information about their country and the world from sources other than the regime itself. Still, the Soviet Union remained a country where all political life was controlled by one political party. The party/state retained total control over the economy. No truth other than that of the Communist party reached the people through the media, which remained completely under party control. From Stalin's death up to and including Mikhail Gorbachev's rise to power, the Communist party chose all the country's leaders and determined all its policies, leaving the population as a whole with no voice in how their country was run. The Soviet Union remained a totalitarian society into the 1980s, although it became one where life was far more bearable than it had been in the past.

THE LAND

The Union of Soviet Socialist Republics was the largest country in the world, the giant among the world's nations. With an area of over 8.5 million square miles, the Soviet Union was larger than the combined size of Canada and China, its two nearest competitors, and almost two and one-half times the size of the United States. The Soviet Union's western border was the geographic center of Europe; its eastern border was at the edge of Asia almost 6,000 miles away. Its territory extended north to south from icy rocks in the Arctic Ocean to baking sand in the deserts of Central Asia. The western part of the country occupied half of the continent of Europe; the eastern part covered half of Asia.

The Soviet Union's borders were the longest in the world. They touched twelve countries, more than any other nation. To the west were Norway, Finland, Poland, Czechoslovakia, Hungary, and Romania. Turkey, Iran, and Afghanistan lay to the south. China, Mongolia, and North Korea were to the southeast. In addition, the Soviet Union was a close neighbor of the United States. In the Bering Strait, which separates Asia from North America, only two miles of water separates the islands, one owned by the United States and the other by the Soviet Union.

This vast expanse that once housed the Russian Empire and then the Soviet Union contains many of the diverse wonders of nature. It is a land of scrubby grasses and majestic forests, snow-covered mountains and burning deserts, deep freshwater lakes and shallow saltwater seas, rushing rivers and stagnant marshlands, barren arctic islands and lush subtropical peninsulas. Mt. Elbrus, the highest point in Europe, is in the Soviet Union; so is Europe's lowest point, the subsealevel Caspian Depression where the Volga River flows into the Caspian Sea. And the temperature of the air varies as much as the altitude of the land. In Verkhoyansk, in the northeast corner of Siberia in the Asian part of the country known as Siberia, the average July temperature of 61 degrees Fahrenheit is fully 115 degrees higher than the minus 54 degree average temperature in January.

Most of the territory that once was the Soviet Union and today is the Commonwealth of Independent States lies on the central and eastern parts of the great Eurasian plain that stretches from Western Europe deep into Asia. This enormous expanse of prairie and rolling hills, the largest feature of its kind on the globe, is broken only by a low mountain range called the Urals. Barely more than a line of high hills averaging about 4,000 feet, the Urals mark the border between Asia and Europe. The European part of the plain is blessed with a magnificent river system that for centuries was the region's main highway. The rivers that played the most important transportation role are the historic Dnieper, the fabled Don, and the mighty Volga. All rise in the central or northern part of the plain and flow toward seas in the south. In Asia, flowing northward into the Arctic Ocean, are more great rivers, the most important of which are the Ob, the Yenisey, and the Lena.

The Central and Eastern portion of the Eurasian plain is divided into three main vegetation zones. In the north, just below the Arctic Ocean, is a belt of semi-frozen grassland called the tundra. In the center is the *taiga*, the largest forest in the world, containing 20 percent of the world's timber resources. Most of the southern part of the plain is the steppe, a windswept, dry prairie that contains the region's richest soil. The Eurasian plain also has deserts along its southernmost reaches in Asia. A string of mountain ranges, from the picturesque Caucasus in Europe to the towering Pamirs and several other ranges in Asia, help mark the Eurasian plain's southern boundary. The plain also touches the Baltic Sea in the northwest and the Black Sea in the southwest, where Europe and Asia meet. The Caspian Sea, the world's largest inland body of water, lies east of the Caucasus Mountains. The Aral Sea, a shallow salt lake like the Caspian Sea, is slightly farther east. The largest freshwater lakes are Ladoga, in the northwest near Finland; Balkhash, in Central Asia; and Baikal in Siberia. Lake

Baikal, a 7,000-foot-deep, sickle-shaped gash in the dense Siberian forest, is the oldest and deepest lake in the world, and the world's largest single source of fresh water. It holds more water than all the North American Great Lakes combined.

Overwhelming in size and potential, the territory that belonged first to Russia and then to the Soviet Union nonetheless is a hard land that demands sacrifices from those who live there. Despite its expanse, it is at once too far north and east. Most of the country lies north of the continental United States; Moscow, formerly the Soviet Union's capital, is at the same latitude as Sitka, Alaska. The country is also too far east to benefit from the Gulf Stream breezes that sweep in from the Atlantic Ocean and bring moisture and warming air to Western Europe. The result is a severe and extreme climate. Winters are a long, frigid ordeal. Summers are short and hot. In addition, most of the rain falls on the poor, thin forest soils of the north, while the deep rich black earth in the south must get by with inadequate or poorly timed showers. Finally, although this vast territory has more natural resources than any other country—from coal, oil, and natural gas, to gold, iron, manganese, and diamonds—many of them were for centuries beyond reach. Only modern technology has made them exploitable.

THE PEOPLE

The population that lives within the borders of the former Soviet Union is as varied as the region's geography. Just over half of its 290 million people are Russians, or Great Russians as they are called to distinguish them from two closely related peoples. The Great Russians were the builders of an empire that over centuries of conquest came to include more than one hundred other nationalities before it collapsed in 1917 and was replaced by the Soviet Union. They remained the dominant nationality in the Soviet Union until it collapsed, and are the group to which most Soviet leaders, including Mikhail Gorbachev, belonged.

The rest of the population, conquered or annexed during centuries of Russian expansion, made the Soviet Union one of the most ethnically diverse nations in the world. The Ukrainians (or Little Russians) and Belorussians (or White Russians) are closely related to the Great Russians. Although each group has its own historical identity, they both speak languages similar to Russian. Together Great Russians, Ukrainians, and Belorussians comprised about two-thirds of the Soviet population. The Soviet Union was also home to European peoples such as Latvians, Lithuanians, Estonians, Jews, Germans, Armenians, and Georgians, and to Asiatic peoples such as the Uzbeks, Kazakhs, Turkmens, and Kirghiz. These combined with dozens of other distinct nationalities to make the Soviet Union the world's third most populous nation, after China and India.

THE CITIES

Although for centuries Russia was an agricultural country where most people lived in rural villages, in the several decades after 1917 the Soviet Union became a highly industrialized and urban society. By the 1980s about 70 percent of its people lived in towns or cities. The Soviet Union's largest city, Moscow, was also its capital. Over 8.5 million people live in this administrative and industrial center in the heart of the European part of the country. On the shores of the Baltic Sea, St. Petersburg, which between 1924 and 1991 was called Leningrad, was the Soviet Union's second largest city. It is home to almost 5 million people and some of Russia's finest museums and cultural treasures. Kiev, on the Dnieper River, is often called the "mother of Russian cities" because it was the center of the original Russian state from the tenth to the twelfth centuries. Today Kiev is the capital of Ukraine, which after Russia is the second most populous member of the new Commonwealth of Independent States. Other important Soviet cities were Kharkov, Smolensk, and Gorky in the European part of the country, and Novosibirsk, Tashkent, and Krasnoyarsk in the Asian part.

In its combination of geographic size and variety and human diversity and contrast, the Soviet Union was probably unmatched by any other country. It lends truth to the claim made by a nineteenth-century Russian writer who said his homeland was not a country but "a whole world." How that Russian world evolved prior to the twentieth century, before finally collapsing in 1917 to arise again as the Soviet Union, is the subject to which we now turn.

2 OLD RUSSIA

The original home of the Russian people is uncertain, as is the exact time they settled on the Eurasian plain. Because that plain has no natural boundaries in the east or west, it has been invaded, conquered, and resettled countless times. At different times, the Cimmerians, Scythians, Sarmatians, Bulgars, Avars, Goths, and Huns each ruled a large part of the plain. But by the ninth century these groups were gone, and the East Slavs, as the ancestors of the Russians are known, had established themselves in the region.

KIEVAN RUSSIA

By the end of the ninth century an East Slavic state had developed in what today is Belarus, Ukraine, and the western part of Russia between the Baltic and Black seas. Its center was the city of Kiev on the Dnieper River. The Kievan state was a loosely organized federation of city-states, each ruled by a prince of the Varangian dynasty, although at times the prince of Kiev was able to assert his authority over his fellow princes. While most of Kievan Russia's inhabitants were free peasant farmers, there were also city dwellers, a small ruling class of princes and nobles, and some slaves. It had a prosperous economy based mainly on agriculture and trade, as Kiev and the other East Slavic city-states lay on the river network that in those days connected Europe with the Middle East and Asia. At its peak, Kievan Russia may have had a population as high as seven million people.

The wealthiest and culturally most advanced society among Kievan Russia's neighbors was the Byzantine Empire to the south. Its capital, Constantinople, was the largest and most cultured city in all of Europe. The East Slavs traded extensively with the Byzantines, and through these and other contacts absorbed many skills and important parts of what became their cultural heritage. The most significant cultural import was the religion of the Byzantine Empire: Greek Orthodox Christianity. In A.D. 988, when the Kievan Prince Vladimir converted, it became the official religion of the Kievan state. This event was enormously important because of the split between the Greek Orthodox church in Constantinople and the Roman Catholic church in Rome that occurred in 1054. The East Slavs remained faithful to Orthodoxy, which helped drive a wedge between them and most of Europe to the west, which followed Roman Catholicism.

Power in Kievan Russia was divided between the princes, the nobility, and the city councils (called *veches*), although their relative strengths varied from city to city and region to region. Kievan accomplishments—from literature, art, and architecture to government and law—rivaled those in most other European societies. Kiev itself had a population of over 100,000 and its St.

Sophia Cathedral was one of the most beautiful churches in the world.

Kiev's decline, which began in the twelfth century, had several causes. Its economy was weakened when Western Europeans were able to reestablish the Mediterranean Sea trade route to the east. Constant rivalry and fighting among the Kievan princes further weakened the country. In addition, Kiev faced a growing outside threat from nomadic tribes from inner Asia. In the thirteenth century, the Kievan states were overwhelmed and the country laid waste by the mightiest and most fearful of those nomads: the Mongols, the merciless conquerers of China and Persia and the builders of the largest empire in history. They and their descendants, whom the Russians called Tatars, would control and plague Russia for the next 250 years.

RUSSIA AND THE MONGOLS

When the Russian people speak of the worst periods in their history, they mention two eras: the Nazi invasion and occupation of 1941–1945 and the Mongol/Tatar invasion and its aftermath. The Mongol conquest brought terrible destruction to the country and great hardship and suffering in the centuries that followed. Mongol policy in the conquered Kievan lands was to rule indirectly through local princes who did their bidding. But even though the Mongols ruled from afar, their extremely high taxation and other harsh policies impoverished the people and the land. Because ties with the West and Byzantium were reduced, trade with the outside world declined, and with it the cities that had been an important part of Kievan Russia. An important change also took place in the country's political system. The Mongols' ruler, or *khan*, held absolute power and the

Mongols brought some of their methods to the conquered land. Under Mongol rule, the *veches* virtually disappeared and the nobles were weakened, while the power of the princes who served the *khan* grew enormously. This marked an important stage in the evolution of a highly centralized form of government that later became the Russian autocracy. Finally, during the Mongol era the East Slavs were divided into three groups, depending upon who ruled them. The largest group, under Mongol control, became today's Great Russians. Today's Ukrainians and Belorussians evolved under Polish or Lithuanian control.

MOSCOW AND THE RUSSIAN AUTOCRACY

During the era of Mongol/Tatar rule, some Russian principalities expanded at the expense of others. The most successful of them was called Muscovy. Its center was Moscow, a city that had been only an insignificant village in Kievan times. Muscovy had two major advantages. First, it was located near the sources of the Volga and Oka rivers, which helped make it a center for trade between the various regions of Russia. Second, its princes proved the most skilled at getting along with the Tatar *khan*, and so were favored by him over the rulers of the other Russian principalities. As a result, despite powerful enemies, Moscow grew in strength. Gradually it conquered other Russian principalities. Eventually, in 1480, it became strong enough to overthrow the rule of the hated Tatars. Thereafter, the history of Muscovy became the history of Russia.

The prince of Moscow who reestablished his country's independence from the Tatars was Ivan III, who is known as Ivan the Great. During his reign, which lasted from 1462 to 1505, Ivan greatly strengthened his power by eliminating the remaining *veches* in his realm and weakening the power of the nobility. Ivan's grandson, Ivan IV, who ruled from 1533 to 1584 and continued the work of building up the power of the Russian monarchy, is better known as Ivan the Terrible. This extraordinary and immensely cruel man has cast his shadow over Russia for more than 400 years. He was determined to reach his goals at any cost, regardless of the suffering he caused the Russian people. Ivan completely smashed the remaining power of the nobility. His most important weapon was Russia's first political police, called the *oprichnia*, which Ivan used to wage a reign of terror that lasted many years. Not satisfied with being a mere prince, Ivan had himself crowned Tsar (Russian for Caesar) of "all the Russias" in 1547. More than any other Russian ruler, he was responsible for building the Russian autocracy that dominated Russian life until the twentieth century. In one sense that autocracy was an important source of Russian power, because it could command all the country's resources to feed its military machine. At the same time, the Russian autocracy crippled individual initiative, and therefore was a major cause of the country's weakness.

OLD RUSSIA'S MAJOR PROBLEMS

The years after Ivan the Terrible's death were troubled ones. The old royal line had died out, leading to a succession crisis and a struggle for the throne. There were invasions and rebellions that threatened the Russian state's survival. But Russia and its autocracy survived these troubles. A new dynasty, the Romanovs, was established in 1613. By the end of the seventeenth century the autocracy had almost complete control over the Russian people. Although it had extended Russia's size and power by rapid expansion in Asia, Russia still faced some serious problems it could not solve.

The first of these was *serfdom*. Russian serfdom had similarities to European serfdom and American slavery, but was different from both. No single law created Russian serfdom. Instead, the autocracy issued a series of decrees over many years that gradually turned the free peasants into serfs. The problem was that Russia had huge open spaces in the southern and eastern parts of the country to which dissatisfied peasants could flee if they were bold enough to take the chance. This deprived the nobles of the labor they needed on their estates and denied the government taxpaying peasants and recruits for the army.

Serfdom developed during the sixteenth and early seventeenth centuries and eventually held the great majority of Russian people in its grip. Like the European serfs, Russian serfs were bound to the land, had to work long hours for their landlords, and owed the government heavy taxes. Like American slaves, Russian serfs could be sold, frequently without their families. In addition, Russian serfs could be conscripted into the army for a term of twenty-five years. If they violated the strict rules that governed their lives, they were subject to harsh punishment from both their landlords and the state.

Serfdom solved the problems of landlords, tax collectors, and the army, but at a very high price. It was a cruel and brutalizing institution. The peasants were under control—except when they rose periodically in violent rebellion—but they also were ignorant, demoralized, and inefficient farmers. Because most Russians were peasants, and the peasants were poverty-stricken and barely able to survive, Russia itself was poor and seething with discontent. Already in the eighteenth century a few enlightened Russians were beginning to question serfdom on both moral and practical grounds. By the nineteenth century, most educated Russians understood that serfdom was a brutal and inefficient system that was weakening the country.

Serfdom actually was both the cause and a part of an even greater problem facing Russia: economic and technical backwardness. In Europe, the end of the Middle Ages brought economic progress, scientific discoveries, and political changes that both improved the standard of living in the many countries and increased their military power. Russian rulers were aware of these developments as early as the sixteenth century and occasionally hired Western technical specialists, especially those who could improve the army. However, as Europe advanced even faster during the seventeenth and eighteenth centuries, Russia fell further behind. Russia was being held back by the deadening weights of autocracy and serfdom, both of which crushed the individual initiative that encouraged progress. However, not until the nineteenth century was it permissable to criticize serfdom. Those who spoke against the autocracy risked severe punishment even after 1800.

EARLY ATTEMPTS AT MODERNIZATION

The first tsar who attempted to deal systematically with Russian backwardness was Peter I (1689–1725), also known as Peter the Great. Peter's immediate concern was to strengthen the army for his wars against Russia's rivals, especially Sweden in the west and the Ottoman Empire in the south. He also recognized that in the long run Russia would be unable to compete with Europe unless it closed the technological gap with the West.

There were many Russians, including nobles and ordinary people, who opposed Peter's reforms. His response was ruthless repression of anyone who tried to stand in his way. His program went far beyond what anyone else had done before. Peter did not simply bring in Western experts. He established schools to give Russians advanced technical knowledge. To promote higher learning, Peter founded his country's Academy of Sciences. He undertook the first program to expand Russian industry. When Peter became tsar, Russia had only twenty industrial enterprises; when he died, it had over two hundred. Peter also reformed the administrative apparatus of the Russian government, including creating a civil service system. He also overhauled the Russian army and navy with the help of foreign experts. This effort soon produced battlefield victories and new territory for Russia at the expense of Sweden and the Ottoman Empire.

Peter's reforms, especially his military programs, cost a great deal. As was the pattern earlier and later in Russia, it was the peasants who paid the price. Some were conscripted to work under horrible conditions in Peter's new factories, while those who remained on the land struggled under heavier new taxes. Uncounted thousands perished in his continual wars. The great symbol of Peter's reign and his programs was the new capital he built on the shore of the Baltic Sea. Peter chose a poor site for a city, a swampy shoreline plagued by regular flooding and an unhealthy climate. But Peter wanted his capital as close to Western Europe as possible, and it did not bother him that thousands of peasants forced to build the city died in the process. Peter named his brand-new capital St. Petersburg, after his patron saint. Others, with justification, called it the "city built on bones." A century later, Alexander Pushkin, Russia's greatest poet and both an admirer and critic of Peter, immortalized both Peter and one of the city's terrible floods in his poem "The Bronze Horseman."

Peter's reforms, while impressive, did not overcome Russia's backwardness. He did not change any of the basic institutions of Russian life that were holding the country back, most importantly the autocracy and serf-dom. In fact, he reinforced both of them. This was quite logical, as Peter did not want Russia to be like Western Europe. He wanted instead to preserve Russia's social, economic, and political system by importing Western European technology while keeping the rest of its culture out, especially Western European ideas about government and freedom that might undermine the Russian autocracy. But this also meant that unlike the countries of Western Europe, Russia remained unable to generate continued scientific and technical progress. Therefore, after Peter died, Russia began to fall further behind the Western Europeans.

At the same time, Peter's reforms added new problems. By devoting so much of Russia's resources to the military, civilian needs were ignored, and the population as a whole suffered. Perhaps more damaging in the long run, a split developed between the small minority of Russians, mainly nobles, exposed to Western influences, and the rest of the population. Over the generations, this division caused increasing tension as growing numbers of westernized nobles became critical of conditions in their country, and of the autocracy they blamed for those conditions.

Neither Peter nor his successors ever solved the problem of how to compete with Western Europe without becoming *like* Western Europe. What few reforms were undertaken in the rest of the eighteenth century and during the first half of the nineteenth century ran aground on that rock. Most significantly, no reform of serfdom was undertaken for far too long. This failure overshadowed the limited cultural, economic, and administrative progress made during the century after Peter's death. By the second half of the nineteenth century the industrialization of Western Europe meant the pressures on Russia became greater than ever. The result was another series of reforms that went further than Peter the Great could have imagined.

NINETEENTH-CENTURY REFORMS

After generations of failing to act on the issue, Russia's defeat in the Crimean War (1853–1856) forced its leaders to do something about serfdom. The war revealed that the tsar's armies, despite their huge size, were no match for much smaller but well-equipped European armies. Wartime hardships and the rash of peasant disturbances that resulted also highlighted the poverty of the countryside and most of the Russian population. As a result, Tsar Alexander II abolished serfdom in 1861.

The abolition of serfdom was accompanied by several other major reforms, including overhauls of local rural government, urban government, education, justice, and the military. Together they are known as the Great Reforms. Some of these reforms were reasonably successful, particularly the improved court system. The new elected bodies of local government, known as *zemstvos*, did a good job of improving services such as education and health care.

But the abolition of serfdom, the most important of Alexander II's reforms, was incomplete and therefore ultimately unsuccessful. Although the peasants were freed from the authority of their landlords, they lacked many legal rights and remained second-class citizens. Despite Alexander II's legal reforms, the peasants were subject to special courts. Their worst legal disability was that they remained subject to what in Russian was called a *mir*, or commune, an institution that had existed for centuries before the abolition of serfdom. Although the freed peasants had received land, it was controlled by the *mir*s rather than by individual peasant households. The *mir*s also regulated how the peasants could farm and determined whether individual peasants could leave their land and go elsewhere. As before 1861, the government collected taxes and conscripted army recruits through the *mir*s. They therefore remained what they had been before 1861, a handy method the government used to control the peasantry.

Perhaps more important, the emancipation of the peasantry from serfdom did nothing to liberate them from their terrible poverty. Although the freed peasants were given land, it was less than they needed to provide a decent living. Nor did centuries of unpaid labor entitle the Russian peasantry to free land. They were forced to pay a very high price for that land, as well as brutally high taxes. The *mir* added to the problem. It discouraged the individual initiative that might have produced improved farming techniques and more food for the entire country. As a result, while a few peasants managed to prosper, most remained poor and many fell deeply into debt. The peasants also felt cheated and embittered. They believed their centuries of bondage entitled them to all the land. This resentment boiled beneath a surface order maintained by government oppression, periodically bursting to the surface in the form of riots and violence.

Between 1861 and 1900, economic development did take place in Russia. Many new industries were built, and they provided a new source of jobs for many peasants. But the peasants who remained on the farms received no help, and rural conditions remained miserable. In 1891–92, Russia suffered one of its worst famines ever. Meanwhile, after the assassination of Alexander II in 1881, the new tsar Alexander III undid many of his father's reforms. He expanded the powers of the political police and issued several extremely repressive laws. The empire's non-Russian minorities experienced increased persecution, especially the Jews. Jews were the victims of many murderous acts of mob violence called *pogroms* that often took place with the government's approval.

Alexander III did introduce a far-reaching program to promote industrialization after 1892. But for most peasants, this ambitious program meant still higher taxes, while Russia's new factory workers endured poor wages and oppressive working conditions. Shortly after the turn of the century, Russia was shaken first by a series of peasant uprisings (1902) and then by an enormous series of worker strikes (1903). These turned out to be only tremors foretelling a much greater shock. Two years later a political earthquake—the Revolution of 1905—hit and nearly shattered the Russian Empire.

RUSSIAN CULTURE

One of the many remarkable things about Russia is the ability of its people to cope with and overcome hardship. Nowhere is this more true than in culture and the arts. During the nineteenth and early twentieth centuries Russia was a treasure house of artistic achievement, as the names "Golden Age of Russian Literature" and "Silver Age of Russian Culture" indicate. The "Golden Age" began in the 1820s with Alexander Pushkin and Mikhail Lermontov, both of whom were brilliant poets and prose writers. The greatest novels of the Golden Age, which lasted until about 1880, were written by Fyodor Dostoevski and Leo Tolstoy. During these years, and afterward as well, Russian literature rivaled that of any nation in the world. Russia's most famous nineteenth-century composer was Peter Tchaikovsky, but he was only one of a large, distinguished group. Among its internationally acclaimed scientists were physiologist Ivan Pavlov and chemist Dmitri Mendeleyev. The beginning of the new century brought with it Russian culture's Silver Age. It was studded with such stars as novelist and poet Andrey Bely, poet Alexander Bloc, composer Igor Stravinsky, dancer Vaslav Nijinsky, opera singer Fyodor Chaliapin, and painter Vasily Kandinsky. These outstanding artists were only a few of the many who stood with the very best Europe had to offer.

THE
REVOLUTIONARY
MOVEMENT

Russia's revolutionary movement did not emerge from the peasants or workers, the two most oppressed groups in Russia. Although the peasants occasionally rioted and rebelled, they continued to believe the old myths about how much their tsar loved them. So their uprisings were usually directed against the nobility and local government officials, and were poorly organized and easy to suppress. Russia's factory workers prior to the twentieth century were too few and unorganized to sustain a coherent movement.

Instead, it was Russia's small, educated classes, those exposed to foreign ideas, that beginning in the 1820s produced its revolutionaries. At first they were nobles—the only people in Russia at the time with a Western-type education. In 1825 a group of noble army officers tried to overthrow the tsar. Their effort failed, and harsh punishment followed.

Beginning in the 1840s and especially after 1860, as education spread, most revolutionaries came from the middle and lower classes. The crucial point about these people is what they wanted for Russia. Most of them did *not* want a society with a constitutional, democratic government and a free-enterprise economic system similar to what they saw in Western Europe or the United States. Instead, Russian revolutionaries were socialists who believed a country's economy should be in the hands of the people as a whole and that every person should receive an equal share of that economy's wealth. Some Russian socialists hoped the economy would be controlled at the local level, while others believed it should be run by a powerful, centralized state. All of them, however, opposed the free-enterprise, capitalist system because they felt it caused inequality and forced most people to live in poverty. They also distrusted constitutional democracy as it existed in the West, mainly because they felt that political institutions in capitalist societies were manipulated and controlled by the rich at the expense of the poor.

Beyond that, many Russian revolutionaries did not believe that the people as a whole could make a socialist revolution. There were two reasons for this. First, most attempts to speak to the people were quickly ended by the government's political police. Second, even when revolutionaries managed to get to the people, most of whom were peasants, they found the peasants far more concerned with having enough to eat than with wild ideas about a perfect socialist world. As a result, many Russian revolutionaries became convinced that they had to do the job themselves. They also believed that once they overthrew the tsar and seized power a dictatorship dominated by their group would be required to organize a socialist society.

From the 1860s to the late 1880s, virtually all Russian revolutionaries agreed on one thing: that the revolution depended for its success on the peasantry, either acting for itself or organized and controlled by a small group of revolutionary intellectuals. These revolutionaries were called populists. The problem was that no strategy involving the peasantry worked. As a result, in the late 1870s some populists turned in desperation to the tactic of political murder. They hoped that killing important government officials would disrupt the regime and spark the Russian peasantry to revolt. In 1881, a tiny group of revolutionaries succeeded in assassinating the tsar, by far the most important official of all. But the peasants either went about their normal business or mourned their fallen tsar. The leaders of the plot, including a twenty-eight-year-old woman, were hanged, and the rest of the group was imprisoned.

By the 1880s a few Russian revolutionaries had found a new theory based on the ideas of a German philosopher named Karl Marx. According to Marxism, there could be no socialist revolution until capitalism had developed, industry had been built, and a new class of factory workers called the proletariat had become the majority. Russian Marxists, who called themselves Social Democrats, began to organize small groups in the 1890s. After failing in their first attempt in 1898, they set up a national party in 1903. This immediately split into two groups: one side was called the Mensheviks ("minority," based on a series of votes taken at a party meeting), and the other side was the Bolsheviks ("majority," based on the same series of votes). The Mensheviks believed that Russian socialists should copy the Socialist parties in Western Europe, which meant a democratically run party. The Bolsheviks, following the tradition inherited from earlier Russian revolutionaries, believed in a tightly organized dictatorial group of professional revolutionaries that would take complete charge of the revolutionary struggle and tell the proletariat what to do. They were led by Vladimir Ulyanov, a talented debater, brilliant organizer, and ruthless politician. Later he would become world famous under his political alias: Lenin.

THE OLD REGIME'S LAST YEARS

Despite their talents and efforts, the revolutionaries were unable to organize a revolution. Most of their top leaders were forced to go into exile in Western Europe in order to avoid prison. Then, in 1904, Russia got into a war with Japan. The war went badly. Conditions at home, which were harsh to begin with for most Russians, grew worse. In January 1905, a large demonstration was organized in which thousands of poor St. Petersburg workers and families went to the tsar's luxurious Winter Palace to ask for help. Instead of being greeted by their tsar, the peaceful demonstrators were fired on by his soldiers, and a massacre resulted in which hundreds of people were killed.

"Bloody Sunday," as this massacre was called, infuriated the country and set off the Revolution of 1905. Russia was engulfed by peasant riots, worker strikes, angry meetings by business people and professionals, and mutinies in the armed forces. A strike that began in Moscow in September spread to St. Petersburg, where in October it ballooned into a huge general strike that spread to yet other cities and paralyzed the country. To run the strike, the St. Petersburg workers formed a council. In Russian the word for council is *soviet*, so the new body was called the St. Petersburg Soviet of Workers' Deputies. By the fall, his throne shaking from the turmoil, Tsar Nicholas II was forced to make concessions. On October 30, 1905, his October Manifesto granted Russia a parliament called the Duma with limited powers and basic civil rights for the people.

The Revolution of 1905 brought change to Russia, but it also left most reform-minded people disappointed. Once the war with Japan was over and the troops were brought home from the front, the tsar was able to restore order and retain his throne. This process was long and brutal. It began with the arrest of the St. Petersburg Soviet and took up to two years in some parts of the country. The revolutionary leaders, who had returned to Russia during the Revolution of 1905, once again had to flee abroad.

Yet despite the ultimate defeat of the revolution, Russia had a parliament for the first time in its history, and it passed legislation which improved many aspects of Russian life. New laws protected factory workers and expanded primary education. The government also began a comprehensive program to improve peasant life. The remaining restrictions on the peasants dating from the emancipation of 1861 were removed. Most importantly, they were allowed to leave the *mir* if they chose. Peasants also received some government help to improve their farms. Conditions in the countryside began to improve.

At the same time, the Duma's limited power allowed the tsar to appoint and fire all ministers and keep complete control over foreign policy and the military part of the budget. The tsar could also veto all legislation and manipulate parliament with other powers he retained. Although Russia's economy, especially its agricultural sector, made progress after 1905, most of the people remained terribly poor. Russia was in a state of transition after 1905 and needed time—and peace—to complete the reforms it had begun.

It received neither. In August 1914 World War I broke out. Russia, along with its main allies Great Britain and France, was opposed by Germany and Austria-Hungary. A half-modern Russian army was no match for the ultramodern German army. Between late 1914 and early 1917, over eight million Russian soldiers were killed, wounded, or captured. Civilians could not find basic necessities as the war effort disrupted the economy.

The end for the old order came in March 1917. The fatal events began in St. Petersburg, which had been renamed Petrograd during the war because patriotic citizens wanted their capital to have a Russian rather than a German-sounding name. On March 8, a large group of strikers joined forces with crowds celebrating International Women's Day. When the demonstrations grew, Nicholas ordered troops to restore order. But the troops refused to shoot, many defected to the demonstrators, and the protests spread. When Nicholas then commanded the Duma to disperse, it defied his order and on March 12 elected a "provisional committee" to restore order, as the tsar clearly could not. Meanwhile, workers and soldiers in the city, along with intellectuals from several socialist parties, organized a new soviet, the Petrograd Soviet of Workers' and Soldiers' Deputies. Two days later the Duma's provisional committee declared itself Russia's Provisional Government. Deserted by his army and pressured by his closest advisers, Tsar Nicholas II abdicated his throne the next day. Tsarism was dead; Old Russia was finished. But building a new and better Russia promised to be a difficult task.

3

LENIN AND STALIN: BUILDING THE FIRST SOCIALIST SOCIETY

Russia's revolution of March 1917 was deceptively smooth. It took place very quickly and relatively easily, lasting barely a week and claiming only about 1,500 lives. But while the revolution eliminated tsarism, it left most of Russia's other problems unsolved. These problems involved both the current state of the country and the issue of which direction it should take in the future. Russia's overall condition remained grim. The country was still trapped in a disastrous war, its battered army barely able to fight and its civilians lacking food and other necessities. Its future was clouded. While most people in Russia agreed that tsarism had to end, few agreed on what should be put in its place.

THE PROVISIONAL GOVERNMENT

The reformers who organized and initially led the Provisional Government after the March 1917 revolution were not revolutionaries. They were moderates and liberals who believed that the tsar had to go in order to preserve the rest of the political, economic, and social order in which they had a large stake. They were people of property from Russia's upper and middle classes: liberal nobles, businessmen, and professionals. They agreed that Russia should have a constitutional political system and free-enterprise economic system, both of which had been slowly developing in Russia before World War I. They were determined to establish a government that, as in the West, was subject to the rule of law and popular consent. In other words, with the tsar gone they wanted gradual, careful reforms that would allow Russia to follow the Western European path of development.

Later the balance in the Provisional Government shifted, and its majority became people who believed in socialism rather than capitalism. But the socialists who participated in the Provisional Government were moderate in both their aims and methods. They remained committed to political democracy and therefore to a program that would only move Russia toward socialism gradually. Also, most of the leaders of the Provisional Government, whether liberals or socialists, were nationalists who wanted Russia to gain the power and territory that would come with being on the winning side in the war. They also sympathized with the democratic Western allies in their war against Germany. They therefore believed Russia should remain in World War I until victory was won.

The Provisional Government immediately introduced democratic reforms. It decreed freedom of the press, allowed workers to organize trade unions and to strike, and abolished all legal distinctions based on religion, class, and nationality. It prepared for a national election to select what was called a constituent assembly that would write a constitution. These were important measures, but not as important as what the Provisional Government did *not* do. It did not pull Russia out of the World War because the war seemed winnable. It refused to confiscate all noble land and give it to the peasants, for to do that without a nationally elected body passing a law to that effect would be to operate above the law, just like the tsar. Nor did the Provisional Government move against groups that wanted to overthrow it, because that would have violated its commitment to free political expression.

The Provisional Government's most serious problem was that it lacked support among the majority of the people: the peasants and the workers. Thus they began to turn against the new government when it was unable to end the war or to stop the deterioration of their living conditions. The Provisional Government also was unable to control the Russian army. Its problems were made even more serious by the activities of the Petrograd Soviet. Because it included soldiers representing military units, it was able to order them to listen only to the Soviet and not to the Provisional Government. Making matters worse, Soviets that were forming in other parts of Russia, when they listened to anyone at all, heeded the Petrograd Soviet, not the Provisional Government.

Another problem which at first seemed much smaller than the others was the Bolshevik Party and its leader, Vladimir Lenin. From the start, Lenin was determined to overthrow the Provisional Government and to establish a Bolshevik dictatorship. He insisted that this was the only way that Russia could reach socialism. Initially Lenin had trouble convincing the majority of his own party to go along with what seemed to be an impossible goal. But by the fall of 1917 the Bolsheviks were behind him, and, equally important, the Provisional Government was in serious trouble.

The government was in jeopardy because both the situation at the military front lines and economic conditions at home deteriorated during the course of the year. Of Russia's major political parties, all except the Bolsheviks were or had been associated with the Provisional government. Because of the government's failures, all of those parties lost influence with Russia's workers and peasants. Only the Bolsheviks, who rejected both the Provisional Government and its continuation of the war, benefited. By autumn Bolshevik influence had grown dramatically among the workers and soldiers of Petrograd, as well as in Moscow. They had won a majority in both the Moscow and Petrograd soviets. During the night of November 6–7 the party made its bid for power. Backed by the crew of a powerful warship in the harbor, armed Bolshevik units occupied strategic parts of Petrograd. After a short battle, one unit arrested most of the ministers of the provisonal government. The first attempt to establish democracy in Russia had collapsed.

THE BOLSHEVIK DICTATORSHIP UNDER LENIN

Lenin was the undisputed leader of the Bolshevik Party and its new government. His right-hand man was a fiery and talented revolutionary named Leon Trotsky, who for many years had opposed Lenin but had joined the Bolsheviks in mid-1917. Another important member of the party leadership and government, although ranking below Trotsky, was Joseph Stalin.

The Bolshevik government acted quickly and decisively to secure its power. A land decree issued November 8 confiscated the landlord's estates and church lands and turned them over to peasant committees. The same day a peace decree called for immediate negotiations to end the war. When the Western allies ignored the call, the Bolsheviks negotiated with the Germans alone. After long and difficult discussions, the Bolsheviks signed the Treaty of Brest Litovsk. It called for Russia to yield a large amount of territory, and left the British, French, and Americans—Russia's former allies—to face Germany alone. But for Russia, the war at last was over.

At home, the Bolsheviks worked to establish a one-party dictatorship by crushing all their opponents. With the exception of a tiny socialist splinter group that briefly allied itself with the Bolsheviks, Lenin excluded all non-Bolsheviks from his new government. Most non-Bolshevik newspapers were shut down. The two critical early steps in building the Bolshevik dictatorship took place in December 1917 and January 1918. First the Bolsheviks established a secret police called the *Cheka*. The *Cheka* immediately began arresting opponents of the new dictatorship; early in 1918 it began executing people without trials. Meanwhile, in January, the Constituent Assembly ran afoul of Lenin's regime. It had been elected in December in a free election organized by the Provisional Government before it fell. Although Lenin feared his party would lose, he did not dare cancel an election so eagerly awaited by millions of Russian citizens. As Lenin feared, the Socialist Revolutionary party, which was popular with the peasantry, won a decisive victory. The Bolsheviks finished a distant second. They permitted the Constituent Assembly to meet only once before ordering it dissolved and sending armed sailors to block any further meetings.

THE CIVIL WAR

Although the Bolsheviks won support among the peasants and workers with the land and peace policies, they also antagonized many citizens. Many patriotic Russians opposed the territorial concessions made to Germany. Far more important, however, were the Bolsheviks' attempts to destroy all opposition to their regime and to establish a one-party dictatorship. The result was civil war.

Russia's civil war lasted from 1918 to the end of 1920. At first it seemed to go against the Bolsheviks. Their opponents were helped by the Western allies, who feared the Bolsheviks' announced commitment to overthrow capitalism everywhere. Several advantages eventually turned the tide in the Bolsheviks' favor. They had several outstanding leaders and organizers, such as Lenin, their overall commander; Trotsky, the superb organizer of the Bolsheviks' Red Army; and Stalin, the brutally efficient troubleshooter. To deal with opponents, the Bolsheviks established forced labor camps. A series of emergency measures, later given the name War Communism, kept the Red Army supplied with basic necessities. These measures included seizing food from the peasants, taking over factories, and using forced labor. Many people, including peasants and workers, turned against the Bolsheviks because of their brutality during the civil war. But aided by these measures and the divisions among their opponents, the Bolsheviks, after bitter fighting, won the civil war.

THE NEW ECONOMIC POLICY

By 1921 the Bolsheviks had seized power and held onto it in the face of a fierce armed struggle. But they could not rest. After seven years of world war and civil war, Russia was a devastated land with millions of starving and homeless people. Many resented the new dictatorship, even one that claimed it was going to build a socialist society where all would be equal. In February and March 1921, the Bolsheviks faced a rebellion by sailors based near Petrograd who had once supported the Bolsheviks but now attacked their dictatorial methods. The sailors demanded a new democratic government that would be a coalition of various socialist parties. After a brutal battle in which thousands were killed, the rebellion was crushed.

To deal with the economic crisis caused by the ruthless and destructive methods of War Communism, Lenin drew up a bold new program: the New Economic Policy (NEP). Food seizures, to which the peasants had responded by refusing to plant, were ended. Peasants now simply had to pay a percentage of their crop as taxes and could sell the rest on the open market. Many of the businesses and factories the Bolsheviks had seized were leased or returned directly to private hands. The government kept only the largest enterprises, such as factories, railroads, and mines.

Economic recovery was rapid and widespread. The peasants went back to work and within two years the country had enough food. Industrial production recovered more slowly, but progress was still considerable. The problem with this was that it was not what the Bolsheviks wanted. The Bolsheviks were *socialists* who believed in equality, but what the NEP encouraged was *capitalism* and inequality. Peasants in effect were becoming small business people, and some did better than others. These prosperous peasants were called *kulaks*, and the Bolsheviks resented and feared them. Other small manufacturers and business people sprouted up in the cities. The Bolsheviks called them *nepmen*, and disliked them as much as the *kulaks*.

The large industries were an equally serious problem. Marxism taught that socialism could only be built after a society had industrialized and could produce enough goods to satisfy everybody's needs. But Russia's industrial base was far too small and technologically backward for that, and the Bolsheviks lacked the resources to build new factories. Nor was the NEP helping much. In Russia the usual way the government got the resources it needed was to tax the peasants heavily. But the NEP reduced taxes on the peasants so they would work harder and grow more food to feed the country.

THE END OF THE LENIN ERA

The Bolsheviks adopted the moderate NEP because they had no choice if they wanted economic recovery. In the political area, they continued to reinforce their dictatorship. Any dissent by non-Bolsheviks that managed to survive the civil war was crushed immediately after it. This affected not only other political parties, but ultimately those within the Bolshevik party who disagreed with its leadership. In 1921, at the Tenth Party Congress, where the party endorsed the NEP, it voted for a resolution call "on party unity" that put strict limits on debate. Those who defied the new regulations faced harsh sanctions, including expulsion from the party. A new post of general secretary was created in 1922 to help manage and keep order in the growing ranks of the party. The man selected to fill that post, with Lenin's backing, was Joseph Stalin.

With little or no check on the Bolshevik party and government, it is not surprising that corruption soon developed. Lenin considered this a very serious problem, one he had not expected under a socialist government. He became particularly disturbed with the activities of his new general secretary. By December of 1922 Lenin concluded that Stalin should be removed from office. But Lenin already was a very sick man, and his illness prevented him from moving against Stalin. In January 1924 Vladimir Lenin died, leaving the problem of how to build a successful socialist society to his successors.

THE
RISE
OF
STALIN

With Lenin's death the Communist party of the Soviet Union, as the Bolshevik party was renamed in 1918, moved into new and uncharted political and economic territory. For the first time in its history it had to select a new leader, and this led to a struggle for power. The party also had to decide whether to continue with the NEP, which seemed to many of them to be leading toward capitalism rather than socialism.

The struggle for power went through several stages, with various leaders losing out at each stage. The first and most important of the losers was Trotsky, whose defeat was sealed by 1925. After several more rounds, Stalin emerged as the winner by 1929. Although Lenin had turned against Stalin by 1923, Stalin proved best at using the tools Lenin had left behind to secure his political victory. These included the new rules adopted by the Tenth Party Congress in 1921 and the secret police.

Overall, Stalin demonstrated a combination that none of his rivals possessed: ruthlessness, timing, and the ability to exploit his opponents' weaknesses. He not only won the struggle for power, but built up the power of his post of general secretary beyond what anyone had expected. Although in 1929 Stalin was not yet an *absolute* dictator, he had amassed enormous power and can justifiably be called a dictator as of that date. The dictatorial methods the party had imposed on Russia as a whole now ruled within the party as well.

STALIN'S INDUSTRIALIZATION DRIVE: THE SECOND BOLSHEVIK REVOLUTION

Stalin's victory also settled the fate of the NEP. After Lenin's death there had been a full-blown debate in the highest party circles about the NEP. Some Communist party leaders, led by Nikolai Bukharin, supported the NEP. They admitted that progress toward industrialization and socialism was going slowly, but insisted that the careful, balanced policies of the NEP could get the job done. Others, led by Trotsky, insisted that the NEP had to be scrapped and replaced by policies that taxed the peasants heavily and diverted all resources to an all-out industrialization drive.

Although Stalin had supported the NEP during the struggle for power, that support almost certainly reflected the political needs of the moment rather than Stalin's actual beliefs. At any rate, in 1928 he suddenly turned against the NEP with a vengeance. As soon as Stalin was in complete control in 1929, the government began the break-neck industrialization drive. Stalin's objective was to make the Soviet Union a modern industrial power by making as much economic progress in a decade as the Western capitalist powers had done in the past century. Whereas under Lenin the Bolsheviks had seized power, under Stalin they would build a socialist society.

The industrialization drive was based on the Marxist premise that the fairest and most efficient way to run an economy was through planning. Even during the NEP years, Soviet economists worked on economic plans. In 1929 the government published its first five-year plan. Reflecting Stalin's commands, which went far beyond what most economists thought was possible, the plan called for phenomenal increases in industrial production. The greatest increases were planned for the so-called heavy industries—such as steel, machine tools, and coal—upon which modern industrial society was based.

The plan also dealt with agriculture, as agricultural products were needed to feed millions of new industrial workers in the cities and for export to pay for machines purchased abroad. Stalin and the Bolshevik leadership also wanted to get rid of Russia's 20 million small peasant farms, for two reasons. First, small peasant farming was inefficient and, second, the Bolsheviks considered the peasants to be millions of capitalists who were a threat to the new socialist order.

Therefore the plan called for *collectivization* of agriculture. The idea was to combine the small peasant farms into larger farms where all land, tools, and labor would be shared. This in theory would raise productivity, since with bigger fields the collective farms could use modern machinery and techniques. And since 200,000 party-controlled collective farms would replace 20 million independent peasant farms, the regime would have total control over what the country's farmers produced.

Collectivization was a disaster. Millions of peasants bitterly opposed the seizure of their land. Often they destroyed their property and killed their farm animals to deny them to the collectives. Those who resisted were driven into the collectives by force, sometimes after bloody battles against army troops armed with machine guns. Not only that, but the *kulaks* were driven from the countryside altogether, since Stalin had decided they were permanent enemies of socialism. Millions of men, women, and children were shipped to forced labor camps or deported to remote areas of the country, where they were left penniless to fend for themselves. As a result of all the violence and chaos, agricultural production during the early 1930s dropped rather than increased, as had been so confidently planned.

Collectivization was crowned by the notorious "terror famine" of 1932–33. The famine was the result of a poor harvest and the government's insistence on taking almost all of the peasants' grain for the cities and for export. It was centered in two key grain-producing areas: the Ukraine and North Caucasus. The Stalin regime, whose merciless policies created the famine, used it to break peasant resistance to collectivization. Stalin called his policy "war by starvation." At least five million people, and possibly more, died as a result.

In the end the Soviet regime won its war against the peasantry. Private farms were replaced by the collective farm system. There were two types of farms. The collective farm, or *kolkhoz*, officially belonged to its members, who supposedly were paid according to their work and what the farm produced. In reality the collective farms were controlled by the party/state.

The second type of farm was the far larger state farm, or *sovkhoz*, where the farmers were employees who worked for a salary. What the collective and state farms had in common was that the farmers working them were paid miserably and rarely had any incentive to work. Nor did the farms make their own decisions about what to plant or how to use their resources. Most of these decisions were made by bureaucrats in Moscow, who usually knew nothing about the conditions down on the farm. The result was that the Soviet Union always faced food shortages. The peasants and the country as a whole were kept going by the 3 to 4 percent of the land set aside for peasant families to work on their own. This tiny percentage of the land produced one-third of the country's meat and vegetables and fully two-thirds of its eggs and potatoes.

Agriculture was not the only sector where things did not develop as planned. Although in theory everything was guided by the first and then the second five-year plan, in truth the frantic pace produced tremendous chaos and hardship. No excuses were accepted for failing to meet targets, despite the fact that poor planning often produced bottlenecks and breakdowns. Very little was set aside for the ordinary people who did the work building the thousands of new factories, mines, and power plants. The bitter truth was that the workers and peasants, who under the Bolsheviks in theory were building a socialist paradise, lived worse than they did under the tsars.

In the end almost none of the targets of the first and second five-year plans were met. Still, a great deal was built, often from scratch. Existing industries were expanded at record pace, and entirely new industries were created. By the end of the 1930s the Soviet Union had built a modern industrial base. It had also realized Stalin's goal of building an armaments industry equal to those of the industrialized countries in Europe.

All this was accomplished, however, at a terrible price. Ordinary workers often worked under inhuman conditions, but were forbidden to form independent trade unions or to strike. Yet they were infinitely more fortunate than millions of other Soviet citizens. Many of Stalin's glittering new industrial projects were built by forced labor, as millions were arrested and sent to the largest network of forced labor camps the world had ever seen. The death toll in these camps was appalling. Nobody knows how many lives they claimed, only that the numbers reached into the millions. In the eighteenth century, Peter the Great, whom Stalin looked to as a model, had built his city on bones. In the twentieth century, Stalin built his socialist society on them.

THE
GREAT
PURGE

Stalin's "second Bolshevik revolution" was completed by the Great Purge—an event that almost defies the imagination. Between 1934 and 1938, a tidal wave of arrests swept the party and the country. It was impossible to know who would be arrested, since the "crimes" people were accused of were concocted by Stalin's secret police. "Confessions" were beaten and extorted out of people, as were accusations against other innocent victims, who in turn were arrested and tortured. No level of Soviet society escaped the terror. It reached from the famous revolutionaries who were at Lenin's side in 1917 to hundreds of thousands of party workers who loyally served Stalin, and to millions of ordinary citizens. At least one million people were executed outright, and about seven million sent to the labor camps, where over 90 percent died.

The Great Purge was only the latest of many party purges that dated from Lenin's day. The party had used force to seize power, to hold on to it during the civil war, and to break the peasantry during collectivization. But Stalin's Great Purge broke new ground. Its target was not those who might oppose the party or refused to do its bidding, but dedicated party loyalists and millions of people who were perfectly willing to do what they were told.

Although it was impossible to be certain why Stalin unleashed his reign of terror, the best explanation is that it was his way of achieving total power in the Soviet Union. Prior to 1934, despite his enormous power that in reality made him a dictator, there remained at least some checks on his freedom of action. Other men in the party had their own bases of power, and at times Stalin found himself forced to compromise or postpone certain actions. The Great Purge and the reign of terror it unleashed wiped out anyone who might oppose Stalin, thus eliminating any real limits on his power. From the late 1930s until his death in 1953, Stalin ruled with as much power over a country as any ruler in history.

TOTALITARIANISM AND STALINISM

The society that emerged from Stalin's cataclysmic Second Bolshevik Revolution bore little resemblance to what

Karl Marx called socialism. Marx had expected a society that would run on the basis of cooperation and in which all would share equally. In Stalin's Soviet Union, coercion rather than cooperation was the engine that made society run, and glaring inequality existed between the privileged Communist party leaders and ordinary people. These differences are important, but there was an even more important difference between Marx's predictions and the Soviet reality. In Marx's vision, there would be a short stage called the dictatorship of the proletariat, after which the state would "wither away." But in the Soviet Union the state under the control of the Communist party grew more and more powerful, until it controlled almost all aspects of life in its iron grip. This new type of society, in which modern technology was fused with a one-party dictatorship that claimed total control over people's lives, was the totalitarian state described in chapter 1. Totalitarianism was not simply a Russian phenomenon, as the rise of Nazism demonstrated only too well. It was not confined to the 1930s, as the People's Republic of China proves. Considering these facts, as well as what Stalinist totalitarianism did in the Soviet Union during the 1930s and how it continued to influence Soviet life years later, its development during the 1930s must be considered the important development of that decade.

WORLD WAR II AND STALIN'S LAST YEARS

By the end of the 1930s, the expansion of Germany in Europe and Japan in Asia made the international situation increasingly tense. There were few heroes among statesmen of that era, so nothing was done while it was still possible to deter the Germans and Japanese from their aggressive policies. Stalin's greatest fear was Germany. He also feared that Great Britain and France would do nothing if Germany attacked the Soviet Union. He became especially concerned after the Western powers allowed Germany to carve up the small country of Czechoslovakia in 1938.

Nazi Germany and the Communist Soviet Union supposedly were archenemies because of their different ideologies. This did not stop Stalin from dealing with Hitler. In August 1939, hoping to buy some time to prepare for war and meanwhile to turn Germany toward targets in the West, Stalin agreed to a nonaggression pact with Hitler. Nazi Germany now was free to attack Poland and risk a war with France and Great Britain without having to worry about the Soviet Union. Barely a week after the Nazi/Soviet pact, Europe was at war.

Although Stalin had won some time in his deal with Hitler, the German dictator turned on the Soviet Union in a surprise attack in June 1941. The Soviet Union suddenly found itself allied with the Western democracies (the United States entered the war after the Japanese bombed Pearl Harbor in December of that year) in a life-and-death struggle against Germany. After four years of intense fighting and dreadful losses—the Soviet Union suffered at least 20 million dead—the Soviets and the Western democracies finally defeated Germany in 1945.

The upheavals caused by World War II dramatically increased the Soviet Union's international power. Germany and Japan, respectively the main threats to the Soviets on its western and eastern flanks, were defeated and occupied. France and Great Britain, Europe's two other major powers, had been greatly weakened by the war, even though they were on the winning side. In addition, the fortunes of war added to Soviet territory and gave it great influence beyond its borders. In 1940, as part of its deal with Germany, the Soviet Union had annexed the small Baltic states of Lithuania, Latvia, and Estonia, all of which once had been part of the Russian

Empire. The advance of the Red Army in 1944 and 1945 put the Soviets in control of most of Eastern Europe. By 1948 Poland, Hungary, Czechoslovakia, Romania, and Bulgaria had Communist governments dominated by the Soviets. Stalin later set up another puppet Communist government in the eastern part of Germany, which his troops occupied. Communist governments also ruled in Albania, which was friendly to the Soviet Union, and Yugoslavia, where after 1948 the regime was independent of Soviet control.

But the price of the empire proved to be high. Soviet control of Eastern Europe angered and frightened the Western democracies. They had not defeated the Germans to turn a large part of Europe over to the Russians. They also feared the rapid growth of power that the Soviets' control over Eastern Europe represented. The result was what is known as the Cold War, a forty-five year period of tension between the Soviets and the West. The Soviet Union's main rival was the United States. These two military giants, who became known as the world's "superpowers," engaged in an incredibly expensive arms race from the 1940s through the 1980s. The enormous expense of building both nuclear and conventional weapons left neither nation safer and both much poorer.

Meanwhile, Stalin did little to ease the pain of his war-torn country. His last years were filled with plots and purges, deadly campaigns against intellectuals and the country's Jewish community, and harsh economic policies. He finally died in March of 1953 while planning yet another purge. Stalin was gone, but the impact of his policies on the lives of the Soviet people was far from over.

KHRUSHCHEV AND BREZHNEV
REFORM AND REACTION UNDER SOCIALISM

Stalin's death led to a struggle for power among his top lieutenants. After several years that contest was won by a dark horse candidate: Nikita Sergeyevich Khrushchev. Khrushchev's emergence was a surprise because he was not as close to Stalin or as well known as several of his rivals. He was a rough, poorly educated man of peasant background who had worked as a mechanic in the mining industry before the Bolshevik Revolution. His rise in the party ranks had come under Stalin, and he had faithfully carried out many of Stalin's harshest orders. Khrushchev therefore was not a man from whom a great deal of imagination or change was expected.

Yet there would be a great deal of change—and it began almost immediately after Stalin died, while the struggle for power was going on. It began so quickly because, despite their many disagreements, all the men around Stalin knew that certain intolerable aspects of Soviet life could not continue. Under Stalin's rule by terror nobody had been safe, from the ordinary worker to the highest official. The secret police could and did arrest anyone without notice. Within months of Stalin's death, his secret police chief and many other secret police officials were arrested. Some were executed.

Important changes were taking place in Soviet life. Stalin's successors were reducing the power of the secret police under the control of the party leadership as a whole. This would help prevent the rise of another dictator like Stalin, and thereby guarantee their personal safety. Ordinary people benefited as well. After 1953, those who obeyed the rules were safe from arrest. People could not say or do what they wanted, but at least they were safe if they accepted the rule of the Communist party and did as they were told. These changes, even if they did not make life in the Soviet Union joyful, at least made it bearable.

Another change that began right away was an attempt to improve the miserably low Soviet standard of living. Stalin's successors, even as they struggled against one another, feared the Soviet people. They knew that if they curbed Stalin's terror, they would have to do something to keep the people under control. This meant that the Soviet people would have to be given something to improve their material lives. Therefore, attempts to increase the amount of food and consumer goods available to the people began, admittedly on a very limited scale, as early as 1953.

KHRUSHCHEV AND THE PROCESS OF REFORM

It is important to understand two crucial facts about the Khrushchev era. First, the great dilemma he faced was to determine how much reform the Soviet system could stand without being undermined. One of Khrushchev's problems was that there was no agreement on this issue. Many of his associates feared almost any changes beyond those taken right after Stalin's death. So aside from having to determine what to do, Khrushchev faced great opposition when he tried to do it.

Second, the opposition to Khrushchev is important because he never held the power that Stalin did. Others also held power, precisely because none of the Soviet Union's new leaders wanted another Stalin to emerge and threaten them all. This meant Khrushchev needed their support to maintain his position and put his programs into practice. He therefore often had to modify and even to reverse reform policies that he supported.

REFORMS UNDER KHRUSHCHEV

Khrushchev's first and most basic reform grew out of the struggle for power, which went through two stages: the first ending in 1955 and the second in 1957. In both cases Khrushchev did not kill or imprison his opponents, as Stalin had done. Instead, they were simply demoted or retired completely from politics. Those who were retired lived comfortably on pensions the rest of their lives.

One of Khrushchev's most difficult problems was that he wanted to push the reform process further than most other Soviet leaders. It is difficult to know why this outwardly typical Stalin henchman turned into such a reformer after 1953. A possible clue to his behavior does exist from his career under Stalin. Khrushchev was folksy and down to earth. While others in similar positions ruled from behind high walls and armed guards, Khrushchev went out among the people. He was at his best surrounded with ordinary workers and peasants. More importantly, Khrushchev knew firsthand how the Soviet people lived and how they suffered. This knowledge seems to have given him some sympathy for the people that his associates lacked and also made him aware how urgently change was needed.

A major barrier Khrushchev faced in introducing reform was Stalin's ghost. Those who opposed Krushchev's reform could always point out that under Stalin the Soviet Union had become one of the world's two most powerful countries. Khrushchev therefore initiated what has come to be called *destalinization*, which was designed to discredit his predecessor partially. In typical Khrushchev style he began with a bang. In 1956 he made a four-hour speech at the Communist party's Twentieth Congress. The speech supposedly was secret, but its contents quickly became widely known both in the Soviet Union and in the West. Khrushchev denounced Stalin as a tyrant who murdered thousands of innocent and dedicated Communists. He accused the dead dictator of costly blunders during World War II. Significantly, Khrushchev's revelations were incomplete at best. He said nothing about collectivization or the millions of nonparty victims of Stalin's prisons and labor camps. To have done so would have pointed the finger at the entire party, including Khrushchev and the rest of its new leadership.

Destalinization immediately led to trouble. Both in the Soviet Union and in Eastern Europe, people wanted more change than even Khrushchev was willing to give. There was trouble in Soviet labor camps, but the real problem was in Eastern Europe. There were riots in Poland that forced changes in the local Communist leadership, which Khrushchev accepted only after being subject to intense pressure. In Hungary open revolt exploded against Communist rule and Soviet control of the country. Khrushchev sent Soviet troops to the scene, but the revolt was put down only after great bloodshed. These events strengthened and rallied Khrushchev's opponents, who almost succeeded in overthrowing him in 1957. The leader survived this attempt and then made one of his most important contributions to reform by rejecting Stalin's brutal methods and simply retiring his opponents from party life.

Meanwhile Khrushchev advanced destalinization on other fronts. After releasing a few thousand prisoners in 1954, Khrushchev closed most of Stalin's labor camps in 1956 and 1957, releasing about eight million people. He eased censorship rules for writers and artists, although several times conservative pressure led him suddenly to tighten them again. The single most dramatic book to appear during the Khrushchev years was Alexander Solzhenitsyn's *A Day in the Life of Ivan Denisovich*, a gripping exposé of conditions in Stalin's labor camps. Khrushchev also worked hard to raise the country's standard of living, especially by increasing the food supply.

Khrushchev also tried to improve relations with Western Europe and the United States. In 1959, he toured the States, thus becoming the only Soviet leader prior to Mikhail Gorbachev to visit different parts of the country and actually to meet ordinary Americans face to face. Unfortunately, Khrushchev also followed policies that antagonized the West, and these undermined his efforts to lower international tensions. Thus it was under Khrushchev that the Soviet Union withdrew its occupation forces from Austria in 1955 and signed an agreement with the United States banning aboveground nuclear tests in 1963. But it was also under Khrushchev's leadership that the Soviets built the Berlin Wall in 1961 and blundered into the Cuban Missile Crisis in 1962.

Khrushchev's policies enjoyed a number of successes. During the late 1950s and early 1960s the Soviet Union jumped ahead of the United States in the space race. In 1957 the Soviet Union launched *Sputnik I*, the world's first artificial satellite. This was followed by an impressive series of Soviet space firsts, including the first man to orbit the earth, the first space walk, the first woman in space, and the first rocket to hit the moon. New housing was built at an impressive rate, giving millions of Soviet citizens decent housing for the first time. Soviet collective farmers were paid more for their goods, and food production of all kinds rose significantly. And despite several reversals of policy, writers and artists enjoyed far more freedom than they had known since the 1920s.

KHRUSHCHEV'S FAILURE AND THE END OF REFORM

Eventually Khrushchev's reform programs ran into trouble. There were several reasons for this: Khrushchev was an impatient man who wanted results immediately and as cheaply as possible. He therefore often initiated policies that were poorly thought out and could not deliver their promised spectacular rewards. When they failed or were only partially successful, resources had been wasted, and Khrushchev's reputation tarnished. An example was Khrushchev's policy of farming formerly uncultivated land in Central Asia, an area previously considered too dry for agriculture. This policy enjoyed some success, but there were also major setbacks. The worst of them were in 1962 and 1963, when drought and huge dust storms hit the region.

Sometimes reforms did not go far enough because Khrushchev and his associates remained committed to policies they had inherited from Stalin. For example, under Khrushchev attempts were made to increase incentive among collective farmers. But Khrushchev refused to consider modifying the collective farm *system*, and it was that system, which denied peasants control over their work, that made Soviet agriculture so inefficient. Khrushchev's reputation also was hurt by failures in foreign policy, especially when the Soviet Union had to back down before the United States in the Cuban Missile Crisis.

Finally, Khrushchev never could overcome opposition to his reforms from people who stood to lose their positions when changes were made. Too many people in the party held jobs that depended on the old way of doing things. One example of this involved the economy. Khrushchev wanted more economic decisions made locally by people who knew conditions on the spot. This meant firing thousands of people who worked in planning agencies in Moscow, and these people therefore feared and bitterly opposed such reforms. In 1962 Khrushchev's plan to reorganize the Communist party made him many new enemies, including many of his former supporters. In short, Khrushchev's attempts at reform undermined the power base in the party that had brought him to power, a dangerous situation for any politician.

In October 1964 the party's top decision-making body voted Khrushchev out of office. Although he was permitted a comfortable retirement, all public mention of him stopped. Khrushchev's great contribution was to eliminate the most intolerable aspects of the Stalin era by ending the terror, raising the standard of living, encouraging some intellectual and artistic freedom, and attempting to improve relations with the West. His greatest failure was to leave the basic institutions of the Stalin era untouched. A single dictatorial party still ruled the country. The economy remained tightly controlled in Moscow and therefore highly inefficient. The secret police, though fewer in number and under party control, was still a central part of Soviet life. The failure of Khrushchev's successors to deal with these problems during the next two decades eventually would come back to haunt the Soviet Union.

BREZHNEV: STABILITY AND STAGNATION

The new leader of the Soviet Union was Leonid Brezhnev, a top Khrushchev lieutenant who turned against his longtime boss. Brezhnev's leadership team knew what it had to do. The party elite wanted security and stability above all else. This meant ending Khrushchev's reorganization campaigns and clamping down on intellectuals, artists, and others who the party thought were becoming too bold in what they said. It also meant working hard to raise the nation's standard of living to build support for the party and to avoid unfavorable comparisons with the West. In addition, Brezhnev and his team hoped to strengthen the Soviet Union's international security. To the Soviets, this meant catching up with the United States in the nuclear arms race. It also meant trying to reduce tensions with the United States as much as possible.

The new Soviet leadership recognized that parts of their society needed to be changed. In fact, once some of Khrushchev's more objectionable reforms were reversed, Brezhnev and his associates introduced some economic reforms. These proved to be short-lived and unsuccessful. The reason for this failure, and that of other economic reforms the Brezhnev regime tried to introduce as late as 1982, was the limit placed on all its policies: none of them could threaten the power and privileges of the party elite. Brezhnev's job, which he did to the letter, was to conserve the existing system. Reforms that might have helped improve industrial or agricultural productivity at the expense of disturbing the system were not undertaken. The Soviet Union continued to rely on its old methods, which became increasingly outdated in comparison to the West.

The Soviet Union's standard of living did rise impressively under Brezhnev, especially during the decade after 1964. Money was spent on farm machinery, fertilizer, and irrigation. Production of grains and other foods doubled in the 1970s compared to the 1950s. This statistic is less impressive than it seems, however. First, the standard of living of the 1950s was wretchedly low. Second, all the increases came as a result of huge expenditures, *not* increased efficiency. In addition, although many more consumer goods were made available to Soviet citizens along with the increased food supplies, the standard of living was rising more slowly than that in Western countries.

Brezhnev did succeed in catching up to the United States in nuclear weapons and in surpassing the number of conventional arms the West had. In fact, the United States accepted Soviet equality in nuclear weaponry in major arms agreements during the mid-1970s. During that same period overall relations between the Soviet Union and the United States were the best they had been since World War II. But Brezhnev's arms buildup was expensive, draining resources from the rest of the economy. At the same time, by 1979 relations with the United States had again deteriorated. The Americans were upset by Brezhnev's unrelenting arms buildup and its aggressive actions in many parts of the world. The Soviet invasion of Afghanistan was the most damaging of these adventures to Soviet/American relations and resulted in a bloody and expensive ten-year struggle that the Soviet Union eventually lost.

Finally, destalinization was ended. Not only did writers and artists face harsher censorship, but some were sent to prison for daring to test the new restrictions. Meanwhile, the regime began boosting Stalin's reputation. For some brave people, these backward steps were too hard to bear. After people had enjoyed some freedom under Khrushchev, the genie could not be put back into the bottle. Intellectuals, as well as members of several ethnic and religious minorities, looked forward to more freedom, not renewed repression. Since they did not have to face the terror of the Stalin years, the bravest of these people dared openly to criticize their government. These people had a variety of interests and often disagreed. But since they had one crucial thing in common—they all openly challenged government policy— they were lumped together and called the dissident movement. Some were people who wanted to practice their religions freely. Others, especially the Jews, wanted the right to emigrate from the Soviet Union. Still others wanted to see the country governed differently. Among them were Andrei Sakharov, the distinguished nuclear scientist who advocated Western-style reforms, and Alexander Solzhenitsyn, the great writer who wanted his country to return to its prerevolutionary Russian roots.

The Brezhnev regime struck back. Although it permitted some emigration, by the early 1980s it had virtually stopped that flow. Most dissidents either had left the country, been sent to prison, or frightened into silence. But dissent continued.

Beyond that, weighted down by arms expenditures and the failure to introduce necessary reforms, the Soviet economy stalled. Millions of Soviet citizens, seeing their hopes for both increased freedom and a higher standard of living fade, became disillusioned. The country's traditional social problems, such as alcoholism, grew worse, as did corruption at every level of Soviet life. Beating the system rather than participating in it became the only way most Soviet citizens could satisfy their material or spiritual needs.

The citizens of the Soviet Union were, in addition, disappointed by their government's failure to respond to the nation's problems. By the early 1980s, Brezhnev and most of his top associates were old men. Their obsession with stability had led them to exclude younger and more vigorous people from the party's inner circles. During his last years in office, Brezhnev was increasingly incapacitated, and finally died in November 1982. His successor, Yuri Andropov, was interested in reforms and promoted a number of new men to the top, including an agricultural specialist named Mikhail Gorbachev. But Andropov, only a few years younger than Brezhnev and in failing health, died after fifteen months in office. His successor, Konstantin Chernenko, was a crony of Brezhnev and uninterested in reform. He was in power only thirteen months before dying in March 1985. He left to his successor, Mikhail Gorbachev, and a new generation of Soviet leaders the task of reviving a stagnant system badly in need of reform.

GORBACHEV AND PERESTROIKA

5

While almost every observer from Moscow to Washington expected new policies in the Soviet Union once the Brezhnev generation of leaders had passed from the scene, few expected these policies to produce radical change. Yet this is precisely what happened. Mikhail Gorbachev seemed to expect to be a catalyst for change that would proceed like a gradual chemical reaction that he and his leadership team could manipulate and control. To his surprise, he was more like a neutron sparking an atomic chain reaction that accelerates with blinding and uncontrollable speed. As a result, within five years after Gorbachev's election as general secretary, the Soviet Union was swept by change that nobody expected. It went beyond the worst nightmares of the leaders in Moscow or the fondest dreams of the leaders in Washington. And in 1991, that chain reaction shattered both Gorbachev's career and the Soviet Union itself.

Although General Secretary Mikhail Gorbachev had

been an advocate of reform before he reached the top of the Communist party in 1985, he still had a conventional background for a Soviet leader. He was born in 1931, at the height of collectivization, in a small village in the Stavropol region of the North Caucasus, an important agricultural area wedged between the Black and Caspian seas. One reason young Gorbachev survived during the collectivization and famine years of the early 1930s is that his family was part of the new rural elite created by Stalin's policies. Gorbachev's grandfather was the chairman of the local collective farm, while his father drove tractors and combine harvesters, a job more important than that of an ordinary farmer. Gorbachev joined the proper party youth organizations as a boy, earned awards for his work both in school and in the community, and won admission to Moscow State University following graduation from secondary school.

In 1955, after graduating from the university with a degree in law, Mikhail Gorbachev and his new wife, Raisa, returned to the Stavropol region, where Mikhail began his rise through the ranks of the local Communist party organization. In 1970 he became first secretary, or the party boss, of the entire region. During the next eight years he earned a reputation for being an efficient administrator who was willing to try new ideas. In 1978 Gorbachev was promoted to an important job in Moscow: the Central Committee Secretary directly responsible for agriculture in the entire country. He quickly earned a place on the Politburo, the party's most powerful body, where he was a supporter of reformist-minded Yuri Andropov. After Andropov and Chernenko passed from the scene, Gorbachev was elected the party's new general secretary.

Gorbachev immediately brought new energy to Soviet politics, which had been dominated by old and ineffective leaders for many years. He was an impressive political figure, the best speaker among party leaders in fifty years. Extraordinarily at ease with the media, he was especially effective on television. Gorbachev could speak without notes and in great detail on the major issues troubling his country. He also had a quick sense of humor and a wit that brought a lively, animated, and human quality to situations in which Soviet citizens long had been accustomed to seeing stiff, robotlike figures mechanically going through their dreary motions. The new general secretary seemed equally at home speaking directly to ordinary Soviet citizens in the factories and farms about their day-to-day problems, or negotiating issues of international significance with the leaders of foreign countries.

The Gorbachevs also added new vigor and style to Soviet political life. The wives of previous Soviet leaders since Stalin's time had stayed quietly in the background, if they appeared in public at all. By contrast, Raisa Gorbachev was an attractive, modern, educated, and assertive woman. She held the Soviet equivalent of a Ph.D. degree in philosophy and made a point not only of appearing in public, but of speaking her mind whenever she had an audience. She traveled all over the Soviet Union and to foreign countries with her husband. It was clear that Raisa advised and influenced her husband on important matters of public policy, something that was unheard of with previous Soviet leaders. With her outgoing personality and high public profile, Raisa Gorbachev in effect became the first-ever Soviet "first lady." Simultaneously she became a role model for millions of Soviet women.

THE BACKGROUND TO CHANGE IN THE SOVIET UNION

Although Mikhail Gorbachev's name would become synonymous with the enormous changes that were about to sweep his country, those changes cannot be understood without first understanding how the Soviet Union had changed even *before* he came to power. As Gorbachev himself put it in 1987, "Our society is ripe for change, and the need for change has cleared its own road." One aspect of that "ripeness" was the enormous and growing set of problems the Brezhnev generation of leaders had left behind: economic stagnation, social problems such as alcoholism and drug abuse, corruption throughout Soviet life, and tension with the West. These problems had become so acute that they were impossible to ignore any longer.

Another reason that the Soviet Union was "ripe for change" was that with Gorbachev's selection as general secretary, a new generation had taken the reins of leadership in the Soviet Union. It was a generation far better educated than its predecessors and more familiar and at ease with the West than previous Soviet leaders had been. The Soviet Union's new leaders also understood how badly their country lagged behind the West in economic efficiency and technological progress.

Even more important, however, was a third factor: the type of country that the Soviet Union had become in the three decades between Stalin's death and the rise of Mikhail Gorbachev. Between the 1950s and the 1980s, the Soviet Union finally made the transition from a mainly rural to a primarily urban society. The Soviet Union's new and enlarged cities were filled with millions of people with secondary and higher educations. These skilled scientists, engineers, economists, teachers, and other specialists were vital to running the country. They also understood how inefficiently the Communist Party bureaucracy was managing the Soviet Union.

At the same time, this new educated public used its education, its access to modern technology, and the cities it lived in to find its way around party controls. In large, impersonal cities, automobiles made it harder to keep track of people, while telephones and duplicating machines made it easier to exchange information that

In St. Petersburg in 1905, starving Russians—many of
them women and children—appealed to the tsar for relief.
The tsar's troops massacred the demonstrators.

These Russian soldiers are captured prisoners of war. The Russians lost four million men through death or capture during World War I. The war was one reason people rebelled against the tsarist regime.

Major players in the Russian Revolution and the
establishment of Communist party rule. Top left: Tsar
Nicolas II; top right: Leon Trotsky; bottom left: V. I. Lenin;
bottom right: Joseph Stalin.

The flower of the Bolshevik army marches through the streets of Moscow in 1917. Many of the soldiers were veterans of the tsarist army.

Lenin (right) chats with comrades at the May Day
demonstration in Red Square in 1919.

World War II Soviet pilots with their fighter
planes. The Soviet Union lost twenty million people
in World War II—more than any other country did.

Nikita Khrushchev, Soviet premier after Stalin, inspects ears of corn on a visit to a collective farm during an agricultural crisis.

Leonid Brezhnev (standing) succeeded Khrushchev
as head of the Soviet Union. He resisted any
attempts to change the system.

President Mikhail Gorbachev introduced the policies of *perestroika* and *glasnost* in an attempt to reform the political system in the Soviet Union.

This poster on Moscow's Lenin Avenue in 1987 features the word *perestroika*, Gorbachev's slogan for restructuring the Soviet economy.

Andrei D. Sakharov, a Nobel Prize-winning Soviet
physicist, was sentenced to internal exile
because he was critical of the Soviet regime's
policies. When Gorbachev came to power, he
released Sakharov in line with the new policy of openness.

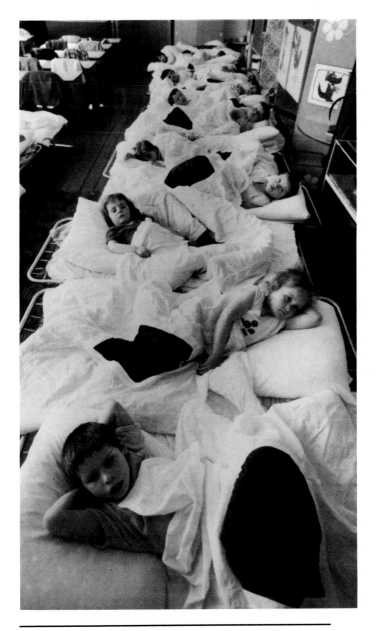

Four years after the 1986 Chernobyl nuclear power plant accident, these chidren were being treated for intestinal problems due to exposure to radiation.

In 1989, as a result of ethnic strife plaguing the
Soviet Union, this Armenian food store was empty.
The Azerbaijanis had cut off supplies as part of
their battle with Armenians.

In July 1987, thousands of Soviet young people gathered at a Moscow sports stadium for a rock concert following a three-week U.S.–Soviet peace walk. In the background are the English and Russian words for peace.

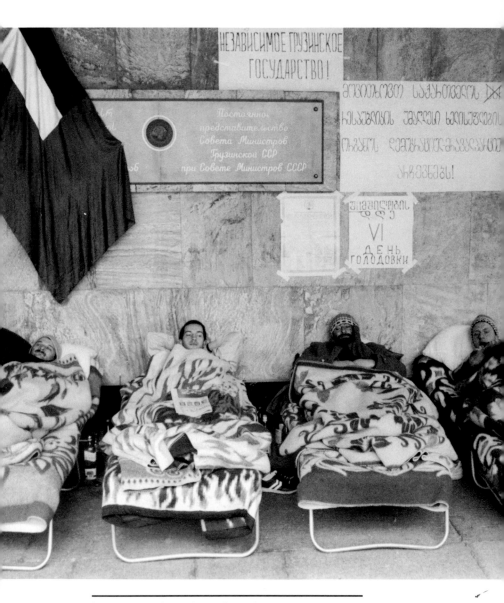

In 1990, students from Georgia are on a
hunger strike to win recognition of the republic's
independence. At left is the independent
Georgian national flag.

In Vilnius, Lithuania, a bicycle rally in
April 1990 supported the Lithuanian government
in its defiance of the Kremlin.

**Demonstrators in 1991 near the Kremlin (left)
demand that the Communist party give
up its monopoly on power.**

the government had once managed to keep to itself. Tape recorders, often smuggled in from abroad, were an extremely effective way of transmitting information without government consent or knowledge. Copying machines and then computers made the job of restricting the flow of information even more difficult, despite official efforts to control the use of these machines. The information that the government no longer could control might be a message from a political prisoner. Or it might be a jazz piece the authorities would not allow to be played in a state-run nightclub or to be recorded in a studio. The information could also be about economic and social conditions in the West, which many educated Soviet citizens began to learn were far better than they were at home. In effect, the Communist party's policies that modernized Soviet society created conditions that eroded its control of a very important part of that society.

Some of these highly educated people were Communist Party members. As these people moved up the political ladder, the belief that the Soviet system needed reform began to infiltrate the party itself. Thus highly placed people began to believe that the time had come to change the way the country was governed, how its economy was organized, how decisions were made about what people could see, hear, read, and much more. Otherwise, the Soviet Union would never be able to match the standard of living of the West. In addition, it would be unable to match the technology and military might of the United States and its allies. Mikhail Gorbachev in 1985 was the most important member of this group. But it was this group's size and importance in relation to Soviet society as a whole that, in Gorbachev's words, had "cleared the road" for at least some of the changes he was about to introduce.

However, if a road for change indeed had been cleared by 1985, it was not clearly marked in the dense and thorny political, social, and economic underbrush of Soviet life. This was in large part because Gorbachev and the new Soviet leadership were unaware precisely how bad their country's problems were. How could they have known? For almost seventy years all information critical of the Soviet government had consistently been suppressed. Covering up information the government did not want to hear became one way politicians and other Soviet citizens stayed out of trouble. The job was done so well that not even the Soviet secret police, the best-informed agency of the Soviet government, understood the depth and extent of the country's problems. This lack of information helps to explain Gorbachev's belief when he took office that moderate reforms could revive the ailing Soviet economy.

The Soviet Union's road to change also was full of deep ruts, potholes, and ditches. Some of these obstacles were powerful conservative forces within the Communist party for whom change was a threat to their positions and privileges. However, they also included millions of ordinary Soviet citizens who, even as they complained about current conditions, feared that radical change would take away what little they had.

GORBACHEV'S PROGRAM FOR CHANGE

The road to change was further obscured because neither the new general secretary nor his top advisers had a specific program for solving their country's problems. Over time a broad strategy did emerge, which was best summarized by four terms. The first was *perestroika*, or restructuring. Although this term often referred to Gorbachev's overall program, it most specifically concerned the Soviet economy. *Perestroika* assumed that the Soviet economy would have to be overhauled to make it modern and efficient enough to keep the Soviet Union a superpower. This promised to be a difficult task. It meant additional hardships for the Soviet people. It also required that many socialist principles such as central planning and collectivized farming would have to be greatly modified, or even abandoned entirely.

Closely related to *perestroika* was *glasnost*, or "openness." *Glasnost* did not mean that all censorship and control of information would be eliminated or that the Soviet Union would become an open society like the United States. Instead, *glasnost* suggested a significant reduction in censorship in most areas of Soviet life, from reporting honestly about the country's difficulties, including corruption and incompetence in the Communist party itself, to allowing its artists and intellectuals to produce and say what they wanted. *Glasnost* was essential to perestroika for several reasons. The nation's problems were unsolvable unless its educated elite had access to information and ideas from all over the country and abroad. *Glasnost* also was essential because the Soviet elite was fed up with censorship. Educated Soviet citizens were determined to enjoy the best of what Soviet and foreign artists and intellectuals produced, whether it be books, sculpture, paintings, music, or other forms of culture. *Glasnost* also was necessary to reach the Soviet Union's youth, which for years had been turning away from a system that denied it much but offered it little of what it wanted. A major problem with *glasnost*, as the Soviet leadership soon found out, was that once a crack of openness developed, it was almost impossible to keep it from widening. Once that happened, the new Soviet leadership found itself exposed to the same criticism it preferred to blame on those who had mismanaged the country in the past.

The third element essential to reform was *demokratizatsia*, or "democratization." *Demokratizatsia* originally meant introducing the concept of limited choice into the communist system. It did *not* mean democracy as understood in the West, where the ruling party can be voted out of power. The hope was that *demokratizatsia*, even in its limited Soviet version, would get ordinary citizens to help the reform effort. This cooperation was essential if Gorbachev's overall reform effort was to have any chance of success. However, as with *glasnost*, it turned out that a little *demokratizatsia* quickly led to demands for more. These demands proved hard to resist and led to changes far beyond what the new Soviet leadership had expected or desired.

Finally, foreign policy demanded what Gorbachev called *novoye myshlenia*, or "new thinking." Since the founding of the Soviet Union, its foreign policy had been based on conflict with the West. Under Lenin and Stalin, the assumption was that the communist and capitalist systems would settle their differences by war. Under Khrushchev there was an important change. Khrushchev realized that war in the nuclear age would destroy not only the capitalist states, but the communist ones as well. He called his policy "peaceful coexistence." But peaceful or not, Khrushchev believed that the two systems were in competition and that communism would provide people with a better life and eventually defeat capitalism. Nor did Khrushchev give up the idea that the Soviet Union could find security by building its military might and weakening rival nations. Under Brezhnev, Soviet policy continued to be to avoid war with the United States and its allies. At the same time, Brezhnev conducted the biggest military buildup in history, behind which his country hoped to find security.

Gorbachev rejected both competition with the West and the idea that military might that threatened other nations could bring security to the U.S.S.R. He pointed out that the military buildup of the 1960s and 1970s had not made the Soviet Union more secure. Instead, it had produced a massive American counter buildup. The Soviet Union's neighbors in Europe and Asia had responded by drawing closer to the United States. The most worrisome example of this was improved relations between the capitalist United States and the communist

People's Republic of China. All of this made the Soviet Union less, rather than more, secure. In addition, Gorbachev knew that Brezhnev's military buildup had greatly harmed the civilian economy, as resources had been drained from the people's needs to feed the military. Gorbachev also stressed that all nations in the modern world were interdependent. No nation could be secure if it made other nations insecure. All the nations of the world shared enormous common problems they had to solve, especially the task of reversing the damage done to the environment.

GORBACHEV'S EARLY POLICIES

Gorbachev's first year in office brought only relatively minor changes, with only hints of what was to come. His economic reforms were minimal, and in fact were really a continuation of what Andropov had started three years earlier. Some incompetent government officials were fired. There were experiments at two factories in which they kept a portion of their profits to finance their own development without government help. Several agricultural ministries were combined into one superministry. Neither these measures nor Gorbachev's other economic policies did much to loosen the deadening grip of Moscow's central planners on the country's factories and farms. In fact, the agricultural reorganization did the opposite. The new superministry flooded the Soviet Union's collective farms with 5,000 different types of forms and bulletins that contained eight *million* instructions and goals of various sorts. It soon became such a disaster that it became the butt of endless jokes, until it finally was abolished in March 1989.

Glasnost also got off to a modest start. The important journal *Novyi mir* published a prose/poem by a well-known poet named Yevgeny Yevtushenko, who had been speaking out against censorship since the Khrushchev era. Yevtushenko's work discussed several forbidden themes about Soviet history, including the fate of some of Stalin's rivals. Yevtushenko also delivered a dramatic speech at an important writers' meeting calling for honesty and openness in Soviet life. But, as Yevtushenko himself pointed out, calls for openness were "not the same thing as openness itself." The validity of that comment was demonstrated when Yevtushenko's speech was published, but only after being heavily censored. Meanwhile, two plays about corruption in Soviet life opened in Moscow. The question of special privileges enjoyed by the Communist party also was raised in the pages of *Pravda*, the party's most important newspaper.

The most publicized of the new Soviet leadership's policies was its attack on what Russians call the "green snake"—alcoholism. As with economic policy, Gorbachev was continuing what Andropov had started, only with more vigor. Two-thirds of all liquor stores were closed, and the hours of those that remained open were cut back. The fine for public drunkenness was increased *tenfold*. At the 1986 new year's celebrations, soft drinks rather than alcoholic beverages were sold on Moscow's streets.

Gorbachev's fight against alcoholism earned him the nickname *the mineral water secretary*, a title that reflected both admiration and resentment. But the campaign was not nearly as successful as Gorbachev had hoped. Many women, tired of endless drunkenness on the part of their men, responded favorably. The All-Union Voluntary Society for the Battle for Sobriety, which had 14 million members by 1987, also supported the campaign. But these efforts were unable to stop the drinking, which is deeply rooted in Russian culture.

When liquor was unavailable in the stores, people brewed it at home. Sugar, used in the brewing process, disappeared from store shelves. When home brew was unavailable, desperate drinkers turned to brake fluid, after-shave lotion, and similar dangerous and often poisonous liquids. Financial concerns also sabotaged the anti-alcohol campaign. The Soviet government lost billions of rubles it had once received from the sale of alcoholic beverages. In the face of public resistance and financial pressures, Gorbachev was forced to reverse several of his policies, beginning as early as 1986.

Gorbachev was more successful in removing people from office who opposed further reform programs. This was important, as reformers held only a slim majority on the Politburo, where the Soviet Union's major political decisions were made. Opponents of reform were strongly represented on the party's Central Committee, its second most powerful body. They also were entrenched at the middle and lower levels of the party bureaucracy, which directly controlled every important Soviet institution. During 1985 and early 1986, several conservatives were removed from the Politburo. There also were major changes on the Central Committee, where 40 percent of its membership had been replaced by early 1986. Gorbachev was helped in this housecleaning by the Twenty-Seventh Congress of the Communist party, which met, according to the schedule fixed by party rules, early in 1986. That congress enabled Gorbachev to make changes on the Central Committee. Gorbachev chose February 25 as the day for the congress to open. This was exactly thirty years after the opening of Nikita Khrushchev's famous Twentieth Party Congress, the meeting at which Khrushchev first denounced Stalin and launched his own reform efforts.

During 1985 and 1986 there also were significant changes at lower-level party organizations. By the middle of 1986, approximately one-fifth of all local party officials had been replaced. Meanwhile, Gorbachev's supporters were being promoted. Two strong advocates of *perestroika* who reached the Politburo in 1985 were Nikilai Ryzhkov and Eduard Shevardnaze. The latter also became the Soviet Union's new foreign minister.

These changes did not eliminate opposition to reform. In fact, while Gorbachev began to talk about expanding his reform efforts more during 1986, some leaders who initially had supported him began to question his policies. The most important of them was Yegor Ligachev, who had worked with Gorbachev when both men served under Andropov. Ligachev had advanced to the Politburo in 1985, when Brezhnev's supporters were being pushed into retirement. But while Gorbachev turned to more radical reforms, Ligachev remained committed to narrower Andropov-style reforms. As a result, Ligachev emerged as Gorbachev's main rival on the Politburo.

It was in the area of foreign policy that Gorbachev enjoyed the most success during his first year in office. The new general secretary immediately turned to improving relations with Western Europe and the United States. In August 1985 he suspended Soviet nuclear tests. That suspension lasted for about eighteen months. Since the United States continued with its tests, Gorbachev became popular with the antinuclear/peace movement in Western Europe. A visit to Paris provided the new Soviet general secretary with a stage from which he charmed millions of Western Europeans. Soviet/American relations improved when the two nations resumed arms control negotiations, which had been suspended while Andropov was general secretary. Gorbachev also began what would become a series of face-to-face summit meetings with President Ronald Reagan in November 1985. That first meeting in Geneva, Switzerland, did not yield any concrete results. But Gorbachev and Reagan both were determined to improve U.S./Soviet relations and agreed that each would visit the other's country during 1986.

THE CHERNOBYL DISASTER

Shortly after the Twenty-Seventh Party Congress closed, having provided Gorbachev with a series of political victories, a new problem literally blew up in his face. Early Sunday morning, April 26, 1986, one of the four reactors of the Chernobyl nuclear power plant in the Ukraine exploded. The explosion blew away part of the control room and started a fire with 200-foot high flames roaring skyward. Far worse, it also sent huge quantities of radioactive poisons into the atmosphere. Air currents quickly carried those poisons across the Ukraine and Belorussia, and from those regions into central and western Europe.

The Chernobyl explosion was not the Soviet Union's first nuclear disaster. In 1957 a nuclear waste dump in the Ural Mountains had exploded and turned a small region into an uninhabitable nuclear wasteland. But the Chernobyl disaster was much worse. Unlike the pre-*glasnost* days of 1957, it was impossible to keep the disaster secret. In addition the Chernobyl explosion spewed far more nuclear poisons over a much larger area than the earlier disaster.

One of the first things to be damaged by Chernobyl was Gorbachev's fledgling policy of *glasnost*. Although monitoring stations in Sweden—seven hundred miles away—detected radioactivity from the accident as early as Monday morning, the Soviets said nothing about the accident until late that evening. When the evening news broadcast finally announced that an "accident" occurred at the plant, it said only that some damage had resulted. There was no official government response until three days after the accident, while Gorbachev himself said nothing in public until May 14! In the meantime, the Western press publicized all sorts of rumors about the disaster, many of which turned out to be exaggerated. The Soviets then denounced the Western press for its mistakes, ignoring the fact that those errors had occurred because the Soviets had refused to release information about what really had occurred at Chernobyl. The initial Soviet silence about the disaster resembled the pre-*glasnost* days of both Soviet and pre–1917 Russian history. It recalled the comment by an eighteenth-century

British visitor to Russia who remarked: "Half of Russia may be destroyed and the other half would know nothing about the matter."

The Soviet initial reaction at the accident site was no better. The top officials at the scene, including the plant's deputy director, literally ran away. Government officials reacted slowly to protect the local population. Thirty-six hours after the explosion, children were still playing in the streets of the village of Pripyat, only five miles (8 km) from the power plant. The town of Chernobyl, a little farther away, was not evacuated for a full week.

The Chernobyl disaster could have become a far more devastating catastrophe had it not been for the heroic actions of a handful of people. Initially a fire-fighting team of only twenty-eight men fought the blaze created by the explosion, and they did so without equipment to protect them from radiation. They fought a desperate battle to keep the fire from spreading to other reactors and a nearby oil storage facility. In fact, the roof of the nearest reactor did catch fire, but it was extinguished before it could spread downward. Several of the fire fighters received fatal doses of radiation.

The job of sealing the damaged reactor to stop the radiation emissions fell to air force helicopter pilots, who dropped over 5,000 tons of sand, lead, and boron on the blackened, radiating hulk. These men, working (like the fire fighters) without protection, also received dangerous radiation doses. At least one of them later developed leukemia; in 1990 he came to the United States where he was given a bone marrow transplant to save his life. Teams of nuclear technicians, who at least wore protective suits, had to spend several days shutting down and monitoring the other three nuclear reactors at Chernobyl. But their protective gear did not prevent these technicians from absorbing five times the radiation considered safe by Western scientists over the course of a year.

Other teams worked furiously to cool the reactor

while it was being encased by the helicopters. The danger was that the reactor, whose carbon core had caught fire, would get too hot. This would create two terrible dangers. If water trapped inside the buried reactor turned to steam, a second explosion would spew thousands of tons of radioactive material into the air. Alternatively, the superheated reactor might burn its way into the ground and down to the region's water table. This would contaminate the water for much of the Ukraine, the Soviet Union's breadbasket.

The job of cooling the crippled reactor was done by installing tubes that fed freezing liquid nitrogen underneath its smoldering remains. Meanwhile, aid poured in from foreign countries. It ranged from doctors to treat those exposed to radiation to remote-controlled robots to install the tubes for the cooling liquid nitrogen.

On June 6, *Pravda*, the Soviet Union's most important newspaper, published "Thoughts on Chernobyl," the poet Andrei Voznesensky's tribute to the ordinary men who did their jobs and thereby became the heroes of Chernobyl:

God is a man who,
Though irradiated,
Went into the object,
Who put out the reactor fires
Having burnt his skin and his clothes.
He did not save himself.
He saved Kiev and Odessa. . . .

When the robot failed to switch off the tragedy,
A man stepped into that radiant block.
We both stayed alive, you and I,
Because that was a real man.[1]

The Soviet government finally issued a full report on the Chernobyl disaster four months later. It claimed that thirty-one people, not hundreds as the Western press had reported, died as an immediate result of the accident. (Unofficial Soviet sources put the figure at over 300.) However, the long-term damage was far worse. Almost 200,000 people had to leave their homes permanently because radiation made these houses unsafe to live in. Estimates were that thousands (nobody knows how many) would die because of disease caused by excessive radiation doses. Over 600,000 people, including 250,000 children, received enough radiation so that they would have to be regularly checked for cancer for the rest of their lives. Another one million people had to live under special restrictions because their homes were in radioactive areas. Over 12 million acres of land in the Ukraine were contaminated, including 8.6 million acres of rich agricultural land. In neighboring Belorussia, over 20 percent of the entire republic received radiation from the accident. By 1990, the total cost of the accident— including removing contaminated soil and lost production—had topped 20 *billion* dollars. It was a sum that the Soviet Union, with all its other problems, could ill afford, and a figure destined to go much higher with the passage of time.

The Chernobyl disaster did not bring an end to the Soviet nuclear power industry. Over the next several years new nuclear plants were brought on line. However, Soviet citizens began to express concern about the safety of nuclear power. They were especially concerned about plants similar in design to the Chernobyl facility, and about plants built in populated areas or in unsafe regions, such as those subject to earthquakes. In the freer atmosphere of the Gorbachev era, demands began to be heard that unsafe nuclear plants be closed. In 1990 authorities in the Ukraine announced plans to close the remaining three reactors at the Chernobyl plant. Once planned to be the largest nuclear power station in the world, Chernobyl was scheduled to be closed down by 1995.

Despite the setback to *glasnost* immediately after the disaster, Chernobyl did not derail Gorbachev's overall reform effort. In fact, *glasnost* expanded as the Soviet press became more open about reporting bad news. There were no delays in reporting the sinking of a Soviet cruise ship in the Black Sea, with the loss of 400 lives, or the sinking of one of the Soviet navy's submarines. In addition, Gorbachev seems to have concluded that the time had come to accelerate his overall reform effort. That contributed to changes that over the next several years helped to push the country beyond the point of no return.

6

THE
HEIGHT OF
PERESTROIKA

In the aftermath of the Chernobyl disaster, Gorbachev and his advisers reevaluated *perestroika* and concluded that not enough progress was being made. Chernobyl was a terrifying example of the failure to solve major problems in the Soviet system. Corruption and poor workmanship in ordinary construction and manufacturing, and the secrecy that covered them up, severely damaged the Soviet economy. That was bad enough. But when hitched to the awesome power of nuclear technology—as they were at Chernobyl—these faults were a menace to all of Soviet society and to the world. It was humiliating for the Soviet Union to be criticized by foreign nations for its incompetence in handling the crisis. It was even worse that millions of justifiably frightened Soviet citizens openly turned to foreign radio broadcasts to find out the truth about what had occurred deep inside their own country. Obviously, it would take greater change than had occurred thus far in the Soviet Union to prevent another Chernobyl.

It also had become clear that greater and faster change was needed for reasons that went far beyond the issue of safety in nuclear power plants. The year 1986, to be sure, had brought some good news. Mild weather produced a relatively good grain harvest, and oil production ended a two-year downturn. Several other important industries also reached or surpassed their production goals. But these improvements were very small or, like the grain harvest, a result of nature's chance cooperation rather than the planned and repeatable efforts of humans. Meanwhile, the quality of Soviet manufactured goods had not improved. There was only a minimal increase in the availability of consumer goods. Nor was there noticeable progress in the crucial area of high technology, upon which both military equality with the West and a rise in the Soviet standard of living depended.

Perestroika's problems ran deeper than how much was being produced or how good those products were. Gorbachev and his colleagues began to realize that they could not solve their country's economic problems without solving its political and social problems as well. An embittered and frustrated population was not going to make the effort to overhaul the economy unless its needs—from decent housing to basic consumer goods to uncensored information—were met. The Soviet people were not going to help implement decisions unless they had a voice in those decisions. They would no longer accept the lies and half-truths they long ago had stopped believing. Nor would they cooperate with Communist party bosses who talked about equality but enjoyed privileges and material comforts beyond the dreams of ordinary citizens.

Gorbachev came face to face with all these problems as he toured the country during 1986 and saw local conditions and heard complaints from embittered citizens. At the beginning of 1986, before Chernobyl, the most Gorbachev had done was to call vaguely for "radical economic reforms." By August he was calling for change "not only in the economy but in all other sides of life: social relations, the political system, the spiritual and ideological sphere, the style of work methods of the party. . . ." He went on to equate *perestroika* with "revolution. . . . a genuine revolution in the hearts and minds of the people."[1] At the same time, Gorbachev increasingly criticized Joseph Stalin for being guilty of enormous crimes against the Soviet people. Gorbachev also intensified his criticism of the Brezhnev era, denouncing it as the "era of stagnation."

OPPOSITION TO GORBACHEV'S RADICAL REFORMS

Before Gorbachev was able to translate these words into action, the new Soviet leadership began to split. A powerful faction led by Yegor Ligachev supported only the limited version of *perestroika* that had been in place in 1985 and early 1986. It vigorously opposed Gorbachev's new, more radical plans. Ironically, because of *glasnost*, which Ligachev insisted was going too far, the debate over policy was carried on in public. During 1987 Ligachev warned that *glasnost* was infecting the Soviet Union with the values of Western capitalism. He stated that the Soviet system of socialism was being undermined. He came to the defense of both Stalin and Brezhnev. According to Ligachev, the Stalin years were a period of triumph for the Soviet Union, when it scaled "unreachable heights" in many areas. The Brezhnev years were an "unforgettable time," when the country lived a "genuinely full life."

Ligachev's words reflected the views of millions of Communist party loyalists at all levels. Gorbachev's rival also had powerful allies at the top of the party, including

Politburo member and KGB (secret police) chief Viktor Cherbrikov. During 1987 and 1988 Cherbrikov made speeches in which he accused Western intelligence services of causing unrest among Soviet youth and minority Soviet national groups. The conservative offensive hit its peak in 1988, while Gorbachev was on a foreign visit. Ligachev arranged for a leading Soviet magazine to publish a letter from a Leningrad chemistry teacher named Nina Andreeva. The "Andreeva letter" denounced Gorbachev's policies in extremely crude terms, complete with vicious anti-Semitic terminology, that recalled the language of the Stalin era. It caused a sensation, both in Moscow and in capitals around the world.

As disturbing as the Andreeva letter itself, however, was the reaction to it. With Gorbachev, *perestroika*'s mighty white knight absent from the scene, the old fears of arbitrary arrest and terror reasserted their crippling hold on the Soviet Union. Nobody found the courage to answer the letter, even after Gorbachev returned home. It took three weeks for him to mount his counterattack. When it finally came, the general secretary's response to the conservatives was sharp and powerful. The media was filled with responses to the Andreeva letter, and Ligachev received a rebuke from the Politburo. Still, the conservative objections to Gorbachev's expanded *perestroika* continued. In early 1989, for example, Cherbrikov warned that Gorbachev's policies were destabilizing the country and leading to "anarchy."

GORBACHEV SOLIDIFIES HIS POLITICAL POWER

The conservatives who opposed Gorbachev soon found out that they were up against an extraordinary politician. Gorbachev was brilliant in seizing every opportunity to weaken his opponents. One source of resistance to reform was the military leadership, which was a holdover from the Brezhnev era. In May 1987 Gorbachev got some help from an unexpected source that enabled him to move against old-line military men. A nineteen-year-old West German stunned the Soviet military by flying a single-engine plane through Soviet air defenses. He landed right in the middle of Red Square, next to the Kremlin wall. Gorbachev used this embarrassing event to fire the minister of defense and other top officials. He then passed over twenty senior military officers to appoint a supporter, Dmitri Yazov, as defense minister.

One month after the airplane incident, Gorbachev scored several victories at a Central Committee meeting. He advanced three supporters to full membership in the Politburo. Among them was Alexander Yakovlev, the real theorist behind the ideas of *perestroika*. This finally gave Gorbachev a solid working majority on the Politburo. The Central Committee also endorsed Gorbachev's economic reform program. It called for reduced central planning, for allowing prices to be determined by the market place, and for steps toward private farming. However, neither Gorbachev nor the Central Committee was prepared to take many of these steps immediately, which meant economic reform proceeded slowly and in bits and pieces.

Not all of the Soviet politicians who disagreed with Gorbachev were conservatives. There were some who believed that reform was proceeding too slowly, among them a flamboyant man named Boris Yeltsin. He was the head of the Moscow branch of the Communist party and an alternate (nonvoting) member of the Politburo. In October 1987 his simmering frustration with the slow pace of change boiled over, with serious consequences. The scene was a meeting of the Central Committee. Yeltsin not only openly denounced *perestroika*'s limited progress, but he strenuously attacked Ligachev as the main opponent of reform. The attack was so harsh and blunt that Gorbachev felt forced to break with his former supporter. Shortly after the stormy Central Committee meeting Yeltsin lost his post on the Politburo and his position as Moscow party leader.

While this obviously made Yeltsin the big loser, at least in the short run, Gorbachev and *perestroika* also were damaged. The general secretary now had opponents within the party on both the conservative and reformist side. In addition, Yeltsin's outburst meant that the reformers were divided. It was a division that was destined to grow over the next several years. Still, Gorbachev's personal political position remained strong, especially after he was able to remove more conservatives from important positions during the spring and fall of 1988.

GLASNOST BURSTS WIDE OPEN

Glasnost began as a tiny glimmer in 1985. By 1986 it had grown into a steady beam. Among the previously banned works published that year was a poem called "Requiem," by Anna Akhmatova, one of the greatest Russian poets of the twentieth century. The poem dealt movingly with the horrors of Stalin's terror. Perhaps the most important book to see the light of day was *We*, by Yevgeny Zamiatin. Written in the 1930s, the book was a brilliant attack on totalitarian society. Reformist-minded leaders meanwhile took over many magazines and newspapers. Important organizations like the Cinema Workers' Union and the Writers' Union ousted conservative leaders in favor of reformers.

During 1986 *glasnost* also expanded enough to allow political prisoners to taste freedom. Two of Brezhnev's most famous victims were released from detention. Anatoly Shcharansky had been imprisoned in 1978 because of his efforts to secure human rights for all Soviet citizens and to win for Soviet Jews the right to emigrate to Israel. After eight years of brutal treatment, Shcharansky was released and allowed to join his wife and family in Israel. *Glasnost* also dramatically changed the fortunes of Andrei Sakharov. Once Sakharov had been his country's most renowned nuclear scientist, the man known as the "father of the Soviet hydrogen bomb." He then forfeited his position among the Soviet Union's most privileged people to battle for democratic reform. For this he had been denounced in the press, spied upon, and harassed. In 1980 Sakharov was forcibly removed from Moscow and cut off from his contacts with other Soviet human rights activists and Western reporters. He was compelled to live for six years under what amounted to house arrest, without even a telephone, in the city of Gorky several hundred miles from Moscow. In December 1986, without explanation, a telephone suddenly was installed in his apartment. The next day Sakharov received a telephone call. The voice on the other end, welcoming him to return to Moscow and to resume his "patriotic work," belonged to General Secretary Mikhail Gorbachev.

Beginning in 1987 *glasnost* flared into a glaring beacon, shining in many directions at once. The novel *Dr. Zhivago*, by Boris Pasternak, was finally published in the author's native land, thirty years after it had been awarded the Nobel Prize. Soviet citizens were able to read Anatoly Rybakov's *Children of the Arbat*, a gripping novel about life just prior to Stalin's Great Purge of the 1930s. Vasily Grossman's epic *Life and Fate*, which openly compared Stalinism to Nazism, also was published. In the mid-1960s, when he had finished the book, Grossman had been told by Soviet authorities that his study would not be published for two hundred years. By the end of 1988, over 6,000 works once denied publication had become available. In 1989 came the turn of Alexander Solzhenitsyn, whom many critics consider the greatest Russian writer of the twentieth century. In 1974 he had been exiled from his country, literally forced onto an airplane and flown out of the Soviet Union. In 1989, his massive work about Stalin's slave labor camps, *The Gulag Archipelago*, was published in his native land. Foreign writers whose works had been banned from the Soviet Union also had their works published. Among those works were George Orwell's *1984*, a classic denunciation of Bolshevism and the entire Soviet system.

Glasnost also let Soviet citizens see films like *Repentance*, yet another attack on Stalin. It was only one of over one hundred formerly banned films released by the end of 1988. In 1989 *Little Vera*, a film about the hardship endured by ordinary Soviet citizens, was released. *Little Vera* dealt not only with topics like alcoholism and poor living conditions but also with the once-taboo subject of youthful sexuality. Its scenes dealing with sex shattered the rules that Soviet censors had enforced for decades. Actually, *Little Vera* was only one aspect of a dramatically new official attitude toward discussing human sexuality. Another was the publication of a book on sexuality designed for young married couples. To the surprise of no one, it immediately became a bestseller.

Glasnost extended beyond the sense of sight to the sense of sound. Religious music was heard for the first time in decades in a Leningrad concert hall. Rock 'n roll, once denounced as a "crime," was allowed to emerge from underground. "Aquarium," the Soviet Union's best known rock group, finally was allowed to record an album at a government studio. Without a single advertisement, 200,000 copies of the album sold out within hours. Its sales soon topped three million. Foreigners also got into the act. In 1988 Paul McCartney, the legendary ex-Beatle, released an album called "Back in the USSR." Intended for distribution exclusively in the Soviet Union, "Back in the USSR" immediately became a collector's item around the world.

Ever since 1917 the Soviet state had been hostile to religion. The intensity of religious persecution ebbed and flowed but never died. This also changed with *glasnost*. In 1988 the Gorbachev government permitted large public ceremonies commemorating the one-thousandth anniversary of Russia's conversion to Christianity. Not only the Russian Orthodox Church, but Catholic, Protestant, Jewish, and Muslim religions also benefited from this new tolerance. While all this was not surprising within the context of *glasnost*, there may have been another factor behind Gorbachev's tolerance of religion. Over fifty years earlier, his mother, a devout Russian Orthodox believer despite the official atheism of the Soviet state, secretly had her infant son baptized.

One of the most sensitive areas for *glasnost* to touch upon was history. It is very difficult, and even dangerous, for a government to tell its citizens that much of what they have been told about their country's history was a lie. Yet that was the effect when the *glasnost* beacon streamed into the dark corners of Soviet history. Many of Stalin's murdered rivals, who had been treated as criminals for fifty years, were restored to their proper places in history. Political figures who had fought the establishment of the Bolshevik regime also received more balanced treatment. This included making their books available to the Soviet public. Another beneficiary of *glasnost*'s new look at history was former Soviet leader Nikita Khrushchev. His 1956 secret speech, in which he denounced Stalin, was published for the first time. All this new information so undermined the old version of Soviet history that history texts used in Soviet schools had to be withdrawn. This actually had one result that probably made most Soviet students happy. Because there was no time to publish new texts at such short notice, all history examinations in Soviet schools had to be canceled in 1988.

Glasnost also shed light on what currently was happening in the Soviet Union. Soviet citizens, who for so long had been told mainly how good everything was, were told about corruption, crime, poverty, and drug addiction. They read about the infection of twenty-seven children with AIDS because a shortage led some nurses to reuse hypodermic needles. The sinking of a Soviet nuclear submarine was reported as soon as it happened. Longer-term disasters also were reported. Among them was the tragic poisoning of an entire peninsula in Siberia by nuclear tests. The area was so contaminated that its residents had a life expectancy of only forty-five years.

Even the West benefited from *glasnost*. Western military experts were invited to secret Soviet bases. One of them was a controversial radar station that the United States insisted violated a Soviet/American arms control treaty. (The Soviets agreed to dismantle the radar station in 1989.) Soviet generals also came to Washington to tell the U.S. Congress about Soviet military strength.

Glasnost, however, had an ugly side. The freedom to speak out, which helped those dedicated to freedom like Andrei Sakharov, also extended to bigots and haters. This, of course, is always the price of freedom of speech, but one that must be paid if that freedom is to survive. The most influential organization that used *glasnost* to spread its message of bigotry was called *Pamyat*, or memory. *Pamyat* claimed it was dedicated to expressing Russian nationalist feeling. But in its extreme form Russian nationalism often contains hostility to the West and a heavy dose of anti-Semitism. *Pamyat* issued proclamations denouncing Jews, and its members often threatened and attacked Jews. Although it operated without official endorsement, it was rumored to have supporters in high places in the Communist party.

THE
NEW
FOREIGN
POLICY
OF THE
SOVIET
UNION

Mikhail Gorbachev's attempt to make dramatic improvements in Soviet/American relations did not always go smoothly. In October 1986 there was a surprise announcement that General Secretary Gorbachev and President Reagan would meet in Reykjavik, Iceland. Hopes rose around the world that the two leaders would negotiate a drastic reduction in nuclear arms. But these hopes were disappointed when the negotiations broke down. The Reykjavik summit ended in failure—the worst failure, in fact, of any Soviet/American summit meeting in twenty-five years.

Efforts got back on track in 1987. In December Gorbachev went to Washington for his third meeting with President Reagan. This time the two leaders signed a treaty that eliminated all intermediate-range nuclear missiles from Europe. It was a small step. These missiles totaled only four percent of the superpowers' total nuclear weapons. Still, for the first time in the history of East/West arms negotiations, an entire class of nuclear weapons had been eliminated.

The next year Gorbachev provided more examples of his "new thinking" in foreign policy. In February the Soviet Union announced to a skeptical world that it would withdraw all its troops from Afghanistan within a year. On February 15, 1989, the last Soviet soldier, a battle-hardened general in his mid-40s, left Afghanistan on schedule. As he crossed a small bridge from Afghanistan to the Soviet Union to receive a bouquet of flowers from his son, he said, "Our nine-year stay ends with this." That "stay" had cost his country 15,000 lives and tens of thousands of wounded. It had damaged Soviet international prestige and disillusioned many of its young people, including thousands of soldiers who became addicted to drugs while serving in Afghanistan. It had frustrated and embarrassed the Red Army—this proud victor over Hitler's legions in World War II had been unable to defeat poorly armed Afghan rebels in the 1980s. The war also had cost Afghanistan hundreds of thousands of lives and made millions of its people refugees. But at least Gorbachev had closed what he had called his country's "open wound" and created the possibility for better relations with the West and the Soviet Union's neighbors.

Meanwhile, Gorbachev came to New York in December 1988 to give a major speech to the United Nations General Assembly. He announced that his country would cut its armed forces by 500,000 troops and 10,000 tanks. More importantly, Gorbachev outlined his vision of relations between all the countries of the world. The time was past, he insisted, when military strength could provide security. All countries had to realize their mutual interdependence and work to solve common problems. The speech was extremely well received and raised hopes of further improvements in East/West relations.

NEW SOVIET POLITICAL INSTITUTIONS

During 1988 the Soviet Union's government underwent a major overhaul. Until then the changes in the country's government had involved personalities, as conservatives were demoted and replaced by reformers. In June some real political restructuring began. Old governing bodies were abolished and replaced by new ones. The first steps were taken at a special meeting called the Nineteenth Party Conference. Party conferences are second in importance only to congresses, but no conference had taken place since 1941. Gorbachev's goal was to strengthen the Soviet Union's government, as opposed to the Communist party, which had been the country's real power since November 1917. His reason for this was to find a way around the Communist party, where opposition to his reforms was still strong.

After heated debate, the conference voted to abolish the Soviet Union's old, powerless parliament. It was to be replaced by a 2,250-member body called the Congress of People's Deputies. However, what was really new was that, in elections to the Congress of People's Deputies, the Soviet people would have a choice of candidates! Not since the elections to the ill-fated Constituent Assembly in late 1917 had this occurred. In every other election since the Bolshevik revolution there had been one candidate for each office, who had been selected in advance by the Communist party. The Congress of People's Deputies' first task would be to elect a smaller, 542-person body called the Supreme Soviet to run the nation's day-to-day business. The Supreme Soviet would be the country's new parliament and, unlike the old parliament, would have some real power. The Congress of People's Deputies also would elect a president of the Soviet Union, a new and powerful post that would replace the old, largely ceremonial post of the same name.

The elections to the Congress of People's Deputies took place in the spring of 1989. Both the process and the results stunned almost everybody both inside and outside the Soviet Union. The elections were not entirely democratic. One-third of the seats were reserved for the Communist party or organizations it controlled, while another third were not contested at all. Still, the Soviet Union had its first experience in over sixty years with open political debate. Candidates argued with each other on television, held large rallies, and distributed tons of campaign literature. And the people listened, although often not to the Communist party. Andrei Sakharov, the country's most famous dissident, was elected to the Congress. So was the recently disgraced Boris Yeltsin, who won a phenomenal 89 percent of the vote in his Moscow district. For decades Communist party candidates had "won" 98 or 99 percent of the votes in rigged elections. Now a candidate had done almost as well in a free election running against the party machine. Nonparty candidates also did very well in non-Russian areas. Altogether, 20 percent of the successful candidates were not Communist party members. Far more embarrassing to the Communist party, some of its candidates lost even though they ran without opposition. They managed this by receiving less than 50 percent of the votes cast, the majority being blank. Among these notable party losers were the head of the Leningrad party organization and the mayors of Moscow and Kiev.

When the congress gathered at the end of May, its proceedings were broadcast live on television. After three generations of watching their "representatives" vote in robotlike unison as they were told, the Soviet public was treated to hours of open and heated debate. As Gorbachev correctly put it, "I think we will not err from the truth by saying nothing of this kind has been seen in the country in six decades."[2] Meanwhile the Congress of People's Deputies did its two main jobs. It elected a Supreme Soviet, the country's new parliament, and it elected the Soviet Union's new president. For once there were no surprises: Mikhail Gorbachev was elected with 95 percent of the vote. Still, before his election Gorbachev had to speak to the Congress and answer pointed and often angry questions. In a dramatic moment he solemnly promised the deputies that "I will never allow the things that happened in our past to happen again."[3]

Infant Soviet democracy continued to grow when the Supreme Soviet began meeting in June. Although 85 percent of its members came from the Communist party, the new parliament showed its independence. It rejected eight of the leadership's nominations for the new cabinet. The congress then set up a committee to supervise the KGB, the still-feared secret police. The hatred many delegates felt for the KGB burst into the open. One delegate said its crimes had no equal "in the history of humanity." Perhaps most important in the long run, several of the Supreme Soviet's deputies got together to form what they called an "interregional" group. This group, which included over two hundred members from the Congress of People's Deputies, was the first formal opposition to the Communist party in the Soviet Union in sixty-five years.

ECONOMIC REFORM AND ECONOMIC PROBLEMS

When Mikhail Gorbachev came to power, his first priority was to revive the stagnant Soviet economy. In many ways his other policies such as *glasnost* and improved relations with the West were undertaken to create conditions favorable to restructuring the Soviet economy. But while *glasnost* and improved international conditions brought Gorbachev success and praise, his economic policies ran into difficulty from the beginning. It proved much harder than expected to reform the gigantic, inefficient, and corrupt Soviet economic system that had been basically unchanged since Stalin's time. Instead, attempts at reform caused the rotten Stalinist economic system to crumble faster than ever. The Gorbachev government could not get a new system in place before the old one collapsed. The result was hardship for millions of Soviet citizens and angry criticism for Mikhail Gorbachev and his colleagues.

After tinkering with the old economic system for almost two years, the Gorbachev government finally suggested serious reforms in mid-1987. They were designed to overhaul and limit central planning. Since the late 1920s, central planners had made most of the Soviet Union's economic decisions. They told factories and farms what to produce, where to sell their products, and what the prices should be. Factory managers were rewarded for producing a required amount of goods that the central planners could count. Because there was no free market or competition, inefficient factories that produced low-quality goods continued to operate rather than being forced out of business. The result was an unworkable maze of prices that were too high or too low, low-quality goods that nobody could use, and enormous waste of valuable resources. Gorbachev's plan called for factory managers to decide what to produce and to fix prices according to real costs. Central planners would be limited to setting long-range plans. It was expected that these reforms would lead to plant closings and therefore unemployment. Higher prices also were expected, as prices would rise to reflect the real costs of production. Obviously, these developments would hurt many people and be unpopular. Therefore, some of them—especially the proposals to allow higher prices—were postponed.

This "Enterprise Law" of 1987 was followed by other reforms. Breaking with prohibitions that dated from the 1920s, new laws allowed people to go into business for themselves under certain conditions. In March of 1989 Gorbachev announced a plan to overhaul and to begin to dismantle the notoriously inefficient collective farm system. It would allow farmers to lease land for long periods, in effect making them independent farmers. This, President Gorbachev said, would make them the "masters of the land." The hope was that once they were working for themselves, Soviet farmers would become as efficient as those in capitalist countries. The Soviet Union also broke with another sixty-year-old tradition by calling on foreign capitalists to invest in the Soviet Union. Foreigners would be allowed to operate private businesses, making and keeping profits just as they did in the West.

Decreeing reforms was one thing. Making them work was another. At best, overhauling the giant Soviet economy could be expected to take years. But the Soviet people wanted to see fast results. This did not happen. Instead, Gorbachev's reforms, which often were introduced bit by bit rather than all at once, caused more confusion than progress. When things did not go smoothly, the Soviet government sometimes partially reversed itself. An example of this was the tightening of restrictions on private businesses once Soviet citizens had set them up. The 1988 grain harvest was poor, and many consumer goods normally available were in short supply. The situation grew worse during 1989. In some regions authorities coped with the problem by resorting to rationing. For example, by the end of 1988 meat was being rationed in many parts of the country. Meanwhile, prices began to rise. Soviet citizens increasingly were forced to search for the goods they needed. Many not only roamed their neighborhoods and cities looking for the products they needed, but actually traveled hundreds of miles trying to find stores with goods on their shelves to sell. Many of them came to Moscow, traditionally the best supplied Soviet city, where according to one report they "literally stormed" the local shops.

THE NATIONALITIES PROBLEM

Along with the economy, the Soviet Union's nationalities problem was the most serious threat to Gorbachev and his reforms. Although almost half of the Soviet Union's population was non-Russian, ethnic Russians held most of the important positions. The non-Russian minorities resented this. It did not matter that officially the Union of Soviet Socialist Republics was a "union" of fifteen republics, each one corresponding to a different nationality. The people of the "Ukrainian Soviet Socialist Republic," or those of Latvian or Armenian republics, knew quite well that they were controlled by authorities in Moscow, who are overwhelmingly Russians. (Moscow was the capital of both the U.S.S.R. and the "Russian Soviet Federated Socialist Republic," which was far larger and had more people than all the other "Soviet Socialist Republics" put together.) In addition, in a country with over one hundred distinct ethnic groups, most minority groups had even less control over their lives than the fifteen nationalities had with their own republics. Finally, many minority Soviet nationalities not only resented the Russians but hated each other as much or more.

All this made the Soviet Union a national pressure cooker. Under Stalin's brutal dictatorship, the complaints of the minority nationalities were bottled up. Under the more lenient Khrushchev and Brezhnev regimes, a few problems bubbled to the surface. With Gorbachev and *glasnost*, they boiled over.

The first trouble occurred in the Central Asian republic of Kazakhstan. Riots erupted there when Gorbachev replaced the local party boss, an ethnic Kazakh known for his corruption, with an ethnic Russian. The riots were extremely violent and took several lives. Far more serious problems developed in the Baltic region in the west and the Caucasus mountain area in the south. In the Baltic republics of Lithuania, Latvia, and Estonia, which had been independent nations between 1918 and 1940, the yearning for independence grew into powerful national movements. Nationalist movements called popular fronts were formed during 1988. By 1989 these movements were directly challenging Moscow's authority over their nations. The most dramatic demonstration of that challenge occurred on August 23, 1989. It was the fiftieth anniversary of the treaty between the Soviet Union and Nazi Germany, which gave the Soviet Union a free hand in the Baltic and led to its annexation of Lithuania, Latvia, and Estonia. That day two million people formed a human chain reaching across all three tiny republics, from Estonia in the north to Lithuania in the south. By then, the once-secret dreams about secession from the Soviet Union had grown into open talk.

If the situation in the Baltic was serious, at least so far it had remained bloodless. In the Caucasus, age-old tensions *between* the local nationalities exploded into bloodshed. The worst violence involved the neighboring Armenian and Azerbaijanian republics. Their dispute focused on Nagorno-Karabach, a region belonging to Muslim Azerbaijan but inhabited mainly by Christian Armenians. By 1989 the violence had taken hundreds of lives and forced Moscow to send army troops to restore order. Meanwhile, ethnic tension produced violence in other parts of both Central Asia and the Caucasus.

Most disturbing to the party chiefs in Moscow, however, were nationalist stirrings in the Ukraine. The Ukrainians were the Soviet Union's largest minority nationality, numbering over 50 million. Their republic held the Soviet Union's richest farmland, much of its heavy industry, and many of its most valuable national resources. Although the Ukrainians were closely related to the Russians, many of them resented domination by their ethnic cousins. And by 1989, while nobody dared use the word *independence* for fear of a harsh reaction from Moscow, many Ukrainians openly were talking about a national *rebirth*, a vague but still potentially troublesome term. The ferment in the Ukraine was yet another sign of the dangers posed by national unrest, which by 1989 was threatening to engulf the entire Soviet Union.

THE EASTERN EUROPEAN REVOLUTION

Anybody who doubted the potential power of nationalist feeling had only to look to the stunning events that shook

Eastern Europe in 1989. The year began with the region still being dominated by communist regimes loyal to the Soviet Union. These governments had been forced on the countries of Eastern Europe by the Soviet Union after World War II. With the exception of Yugoslavia and Albania, they were all part of the Soviet-dominated Warsaw Pact military alliance. However, none of the Warsaw Pact regimes enjoyed popular support. They were corrupt and inefficient, and also generally ignored Gorbachev's urgings that they reform. Only the threat of Soviet military intervention kept them in power.

By 1989 the cost of maintaining its Eastern European empire had become too great for the Soviet Union. Gorbachev wanted to use all his resources for reform at home. He also knew that it would be impossible to establish normal relations with Western Europe and the United States as long as conditions remained unchanged in Eastern Europe. The West felt threatened by the hundreds of thousands of Soviet troops stationed in Eastern Europe. It considered the Soviet Union's domination of the nations in Eastern Europe as evidence that the Soviets could not be trusted to be a genuinely friendly country.

As a result, when popular discontent exploded across Eastern Europe in 1989, the Soviet Union did not intervene. Gorbachev did not want the communist governments of Eastern Europe to fall. But he was not willing to pay the price of stopping their collapse once it started. Intervention would have cost tens of thousands of lives and billions of rubles. It would have crippled reform in the Soviet Union. And it would have reversed the five years of progress in improving relations with the West. The Soviet Union therefore remained on the sidelines when the communist government of Poland collapsed in the autumn of 1989. This shock started an earthquake which brought down the communist governments in Hungary, East Germany, Bulgaria, Czechoslovakia, and Rumania by December.

The loss of its Eastern European empire, its great prize from World War II, was not an entirely negative development for the Soviet Union. For the same political earthquake that shattered the Soviet dominance of Eastern Europe also undermined the foundations of the Cold War between the Soviet Union and the West. It therefore created the possibility of genuine peace after forty years of tension, an upward spiraling arms race, and the threat of nuclear war. Genuine peace was a welcome prospect, for after five years of *perestroika* the Soviet Union still faced enormous and growing problems at home.

PERESTROIKA AND SOVIET YOUTH

One important domestic problem that received less publicity than the economy or the minority nationalities—although it involved literally tens of millions of Soviet citizens—was the attitude of Soviet youth toward the new reform programs. Gorbachev and other leading reformers stressed that *perestroika*'s success depended on winning the active support of the country's young people. The new Soviet leaders repeated this often, as it was no secret that many Soviet youths, along with their elders, had lost faith in the Soviet system during the Brezhnev era. As a result they turned to other sources to revive their spirits or at least to occupy their energies, from yoga and Buddhism to drugs and violence.

One important influence on Soviet youngsters was the youth culture of the West, especially rock music. Over the years Soviet rockers developed ingenious ways of illegally reproducing recordings that foreigners and Soviet travelers brought into the Soviet Union. Perhaps the most remarkable were the recordings produced "on ribs" during the early and mid-1960s. Unable to get access to the proper plastic through regular channels, determined Soviet rockers turned to old hospital X-ray plates, which could be bought very cheaply. They laboriously carved recording grooves into plastic plates that held pictures of broken bones, diseased lungs, and other injured internal organs. These X-ray records of human maladies were now covered with the joyful and defiant notes of teenage striving for independence and individual identity.

An underground youth culture based in part on rock music, but also on various other influences, evolved and spread during the 1970s and 1980s. There was no attempt to challenge the existing system, as the youth movement did in the United States during the 1960s. Instead, many Soviet youths simply tried to drop out of the system. Thousands moved to Leningrad, Moscow, and other large Soviet cities, where they sought out like-minded companions. Many youths in the Soviet counterculture worked only when necessary and attempted to avoid military service, which is mandatory for most Soviet young men.

By the mid-1970s, this underground culture had expanded beyond one simply influenced by the West. Boredom and neglect produced gang violence, prostitution, vandalism, and drug addiction, among other social ills. Violent gangs, in fact, became a serious problem in many urban areas. Some youngsters were attracted to extremist political views. Among them was Nazism, although investigations revealed that most young Soviet self-styled "Nazis" actually knew very little about Hitler and the German Nazis. One group of disillusioned young people who knew a great deal about what they were talking about were the *Afgantsy*, the veterans of the Soviet Union's unsuccessful war in Afghanistan. Like American Vietnam veterans, the Afgantsy had difficulties finding a place as civilians in Soviet society. They had fought in a losing war that was unpopular at home, and many felt that their government had not told them the truth about why they and their friends had been called on to make such great sacrifices in a foreign land.

Glasnost finally brought this discontent, long hidden under the propaganda and falsehoods of the Brezhnev regime, to the surface. A symbol of this was a frank and often shocking film called *It Isn't Easy to Be Young*, which was released in 1986. It probed a wide range of problems, from the deliberate violence of young fans at soccer matches to various difficulties experienced by Afghanistan veterans trying to return to civilian life. At the same time, laws were changed to legalize the status of the independent organizations already formed by tens of thousands of Soviet youths without official permission. By 1988 there were an estimated 60,000 such groups, concerned with everything from rock music and basketball to peace and the environment. These organizations enlisted half, or possibly more, of the country's young people. The government also tried to provide Soviet youths with the activities they wanted. New rock clubs and discos opened, rock and jazz concerts were freed from state censorship, and television stations broadcast shows of genuine interest to Soviet young people.

But it remained doubtful whether the government would succeed in luring back to the Soviet mainstream and *perestroika* the young people whom Gorbachev criticized for being in their own "narrow little world, out of step . . . with the swift onrush of life." In 1988 the *Komsomol*, the Communist party's national organization of young people over age fourteen, reported its membership had dropped by 10 percent in three years and that recruitment was lagging. It was against that background, with hopes and burdens that involved all its citizens from the youngest to the oldest, that the Soviet Union entered the 1990s.

THE FORMER SOVIET UNION IN THE NEW DECADE

January 1, 1990, promised to be the start of a particularly important year for the Soviet Union and for the progress made under *perestroika*. It was a time when major changes were expected to take place that would further reshape the country.

Finally the 1980s, a decade with one foot in the old era and one in the new, had been left behind for a decade freshly born in the era of *perestroika*. March 11 of the new year marked the fifth anniversary of Mikhail Gorbachev's coming to power. While that milestone merited celebration, it also evoked exasperation over expectations not yet fulfilled. Mikhail Gorbachev certainly had accomplished an enormous amount during his five years as leader of the Soviet Union. Clearly he deserved the "Man of the Decade" title for the 1980s awarded him by a major American news organization. Yet Gorbachev and *perestroika* had not delivered on several key promises made to the Soviet people, primarily the pledge to overhaul the country's economy and to provide its citizens with a better life. After his five years in office, the Soviet people were becoming visibly disillusioned and impatient for results. As a result, Gorbachev's popularity at home was dropping. In fact, by 1990 he was far more popular in the West than he was at home. A joke in Moscow summed up this ironic, and dangerous, situation:

Question: *What is the difference between the Soviet Union and the United States?*

Answer: *In the United States, Gorbachev probably would be elected President.*

At the same time 1990 held the promise of major changes that would help restructure both Soviet society and the Soviet Union's relations with other countries. At home major steps were expected to move the country toward a market economy, as some stifling central controls were lifted. There were prospects of additional progress toward the democratization of the Soviet political system. In foreign affairs new arms reduction agreements were in the offing, as was the hope that the Cold War itself might finally be brought to an end.

FOREIGN POLICY AND THE END OF THE COLD WAR

In 1990 the Cold War—an era of tension that held the world on the edge of nuclear destruction for two generations—finally ended. The collapse of the Soviet

Union's Eastern European empire in 1989, and Gorbachev's acceptance of that stunning turnabout, had led to talk about an end to the Cold War. In 1990 both East and West moved swiftly to realize a dream that neither side had thought possible barely one year earlier. This, of course, was far more than simply the major foreign policy event of the year for the Soviet Union; it had equal importance for the other nations of Europe and for the entire Western world. In fact, it probably is the most important international development of the second half of the twentieth century.

During the early part of 1990, the East and West step-by-step came closer together. At the end of February, the USSR reached an agreement with Czechoslovakia for a withdrawal of Soviet troops from that former Soviet satellite. Several weeks later a similar agreement was signed with Hungary. In March the Soviet Union and the Vatican announced a resumption of diplomatic ties—after a break of sixty-seven years. A much more significant step was taken in June at a Bush/Gorbachev summit meeting in Washington. The two leaders announced a series of agreements, including one that would set the stage for deep cuts in the two nations' long-range nuclear weapons stockpiles. A few days later, the leaders of the North Atlantic Treaty Organization (NATO), which had been formed in 1949 as a direct result of the start of the Cold War, proclaimed that long and costly conflict over. In simple but dramatic language, NATO leaders told the Soviet Union that "we are no longer adversaries."

The next several months witnessed several other agreements that reinforced the NATO declaration of June. One important barrier to burying the Cold War once and for all was the status of a united Germany. Since 1989 the Soviet Union had objected to allowing a united Germany to join NATO. In July, after a meeting with German Chancellor Helmut Kohl, Gorbachev withdrew his objection. In return Germany and NATO agreed that no NATO troops could be stationed in former East German territory until Soviet troops withdrew in 1994. The Germans also accepted a limit on the size of their army and offered the Soviet Union billions of dollars to finance the withdrawal of Soviet troops from East Germany and the building of new housing for them in the Soviet Union. That agreement paved the way for the official unification of West and East Germany into a united country on October 3, 1990.

In November the NATO and Warsaw Pact nations announced yet another arms agreement. This one dramatically reduced nonnuclear forces in Europe. A few days later the United States, Canada, and all the nations of Europe (except Albania) signed the Paris Charter, which formally ended the Cold War. As President George Bush put it, "We are closing a chapter in history. The Cold War is over." The Soviet Union became an immediate beneficiary of that closing when Western nations began sending it emergency aid to ease economic hardship and food shortages. The United States, which had lagged behind Western Europe in sending aid, joined the effort in early December with food shipments. A week later, the United States ended a fifteen-year ban on loans to the Soviets by approving a $1 billion loan so that they could purchase American food.

The United States and the West also benefited from the end of the Cold War when a crisis erupted in the Middle East. In August 1990, Iraq invaded and overran its small neighbor, oil-rich Kuwait. Iraq had a brutal dictatorial government and was armed to the teeth. It had an army of a million men. Iraq also had chemical weapons, which it had used against another neighbor, Iran, and also against a minority group called the Kurds within its own borders, and was working to develop nuclear weapons. The Soviet Union now joined an international effort led by the United States to force Iraq to withdraw from Kuwait. The United Nations, long the setting of Soviet/American conflict, instead became a scene of cooperation. The Soviets also cooperated in a U.N.-sanctioned economic boycott of Iraq and even endorsed the use of force to drive Iraq from Kuwait, which is what a group of U.S. led nations did in 1991.

Meanwhile Gorbachev received international recognition for his unique role in making all these events possible. On October 15, 1990, the Nobel Committee announced in Oslo that President Mikhail Gorbachev of the Soviet Union was the 1990 recipient of the prestigious Nobel Peace Prize.

POLITICAL RESTRUCTURING AND BATTLES IN 1990

Major restructuring of the Soviet Union's political institutions continued during 1990. On March 13, after heated debate, the Congress of People's Deputies repealed Article 6 of the Soviet Constitution, which guaranteed the Communist party's monopoly on political power. In doing so the congress bowed to the winds of change blowing from Eastern Europe. Perhaps more important, the new Soviet Union had now gone beyond its rejection of Stalin and broken with a seven-decade-old fundamental principle of Leninism.

The following day the congress, again after stormy debate, created a new and even stronger presidency than the one created in 1989. The new presidency included many extensive powers, including the right to declare martial law and to impose economic regulations by decree. In addition, the new presidency was an executive presidency; that is, the president would be chosen directly by the people for a five-year term rather than by the congress or another parliamentary body. The only exception to this was the very first election, which at Gorbachev's urging was done by the congress. To no one's surprise the congress chose Gorbachev as president, but only after intensive lobbying did it give him the required two-thirds majority in the election. As if this were not enough, in September the Supreme Soviet granted Gorbachev additional emergency powers to cope with the nation's growing economic crisis.

Just prior to the congress, the Soviet people had done some political restructuring of their own. In local elections across the country in late March, Communists were swept out of office in many regions. This trouncing included loss of the majority in the Moscow, Leningrad, and Kiev city councils. More bad news for the Party followed at its Twenty-Eighth Congress in July. Gorbachev seemed to use the meeting to downgrade the Party's prestige. He remained as its general secretary and as a member of the Politburo, the Party's most important body. But the rest of the important figures on the Politburo—including Foreign Minister Eduard Shevardnadze, Prime Minister Nikolai Ryzhkov, and key Gorbachev adviser Alexander Yakovlev—gave up their seats. This once all-powerful body became, in the words of one Soviet observer, a "long list of nobodies." The Party as a whole was further weakened when several leading reformist politicians quit its ranks altogether. The most important figure to do so was Boris Yeltsin. In May the unpredictable Yeltsin had been elected president of the Russian republic, the largest of the Soviet Union's fifteen member republics. Now he shocked the party congress by announcing his resignation during a short speech. The announcement literally sent gasps through the hall filled with 4,700 stunned delegates. Without even a pause to answer questions, Yeltsin immediately marched straight out of the hall.

The next day two other important Communists, Leningrad's mayor Anatoly Sobchak and Moscow's mayor Gavriil Popov, announced their resignations. They were part of a group of about 100 delegates known as the Democratic Platform, which announced that it intended to create what it called a "democratic coalition"—an alternative to the Communist party. This in effect meant that they also had broken with the party. All of this was part of a larger trend; during July 1990 over 160,000 members, 1.5 percent of the Russian republic's Communist party, handed in their party cards.

CONTINUED PROBLEMS ON OTHER FRONTS

The Soviet Union's stormy political battles took place against a broader background of other unsolved and growing problems. Minority nationalities continued their pressure for greater freedom from Moscow. This trend went the furthest in Lithuania, which actually declared its "independence" in March. President Gorbachev responded with a variety of measures, including an economic blockade to force the Lithuanians to reverse themselves. The struggle between Lithuania and Moscow went on for months, until the Lithuanians finally agreed in June to temporarily suspend their declaration.

This truce settled little, especially in light of similar actions in other Soviet republics. Most did not go as far as Lithuania, daring only to declare their "sovereignty," a more vague term that meant something less than full independence. Still, this trend continued and accelerated. By the end of the year, all fifteen republics, including the Russian republic, had taken this step. Barely less disturbing for Moscow was the continued violent outbreaks between minority nationalities that took place across the Soviet Union from Moldavia to the Caucasus to central Asia, claiming hundreds of lives.

While ethnic hatreds continued to flare and burn, economic problems deepened. The trouble was summed up by one official who complained that "we have completely destroyed the old system and proposed nothing in its place." This dilemma was best illustrated by Soviet agriculture. Although the old collective farm system was falling apart, by the middle of 1990 there were only thirty thousand family or private farms through the entire Soviet Union. Of these, more than half were in the tiny Georgian republic, while a third were in the equally miniscule Baltic states. In the whole giant Russian republic there were only 900 private farmers, while the Ukraine, the country's bread-basket, had only twelve.

Soviet consumers suffered because the old centrally planned distribution system broke down faster than it could be replaced by the private sector. As a result, despite a record grain harvest, so many crops rotted in the fields or on the way to market that not enough reached consumers to feed the country. By the end of the year food shortages plagued the country from east to west, as did rapidly rising prices. Prices for basic food products in farmers' markets outside the official state system skyrocketed in the last half of the year, jumping by 47 percent in October and 50 percent in November. The situation was equally grim for other consumer goods. *Pravda* reported that prices for televisions, radio equipment, refrigerators, and similar consumer goods would rise from 50 to 70 percent during 1991.

Among the many other problems that the Soviet Union faced in 1990, perhaps only its environmental crisis involved the entire nation as completely as did the economy and the nationalities questions. As bad as it was, Chernobyl was only one of many environmental disasters that the Soviet system had produced over the past seventy years. Large parts of the Ukraine were polluted by poisons from heavy industries like iron and steel. In Central Asia, the Aral Sea, once the world's fourth largest inland sea, was drying up because for decades the waters that fed it had been diverted to irrigate cotton fields. As the Aral Sea dried up and vast stretches of its salty bottom were exposed, thousands of square miles in Central Asia were covered by huge dust and salt storms, poisoning both the land and its people. In the Urals, large areas were polluted by the waste products of gigantic chemical factories. Siberian land and rivers were being destroyed by exploitation of the region's rich oil fields. North of the Arctic Circle, the after-effects of nuclear testing had created some of the highest cancer rates in the world. The scope of the problem was poignantly summed up by a simple question that a Belorussian woman asked a member of the Politburo:

Tell me, please, how are we supposed to live? We are afraid of the water; we are afraid of the sun; we are afraid of the grass; we are afraid of the soil . . . How can we go on living?[1]

CONSERVATIVE PRESSURE ON PERESTROIKA

While Gorbachev faced criticism from reformers for doing too little, he also had to deal with growing pressure from conservatives in the Communist party bureaucracy, the KGB, and the army for allowing things to go too far. Continued ethnic violence and disorders in other areas of Soviet life gave the conservatives the ammunition they needed. Gorbachev and his policies were bitterly attacked by conservatives at the Twenty-Eighth Party Congress. They were led by Yegor Ligachev, who denounced what he called Gorbachev's "blind radicalism." This pressure from powerful entrenched forces had its effect during the second half of 1990.

During the fall, Gorbachev rejected a bold plan of economic reform designed to move the Soviet Union to a market economy in five hundred days. Early in December, he announced harsher policies to fight speculators and black market traders in food. He then shook up the ministry of the interior, which controls the police, placing it in the hands of hard-line conservatives. The Soviet president also warned against continued ethnic disorders, raising the possibility he would impose martial law on parts of the country. By then some observers openly began to wonder if *perestroika* might be giving way to a new emphasis on caution and stability. Others openly began to worry about a drift toward reaction and dictatorship.

The struggle between reform and reaction moved to center stage as 1990 drew to a close. On December 20, Eduard Shevardnadze announced his resignation as foreign minister. For five years Shevardnadze had been one of *perestroika*'s key leaders and in many ways Gorbachev's right-hand man. Along with Gorbachev himself, Shevardnadze was the man most closely identified with the new Soviet foreign policy that had ended the Cold War. Now he not only had resigned, but issued a dire warning: "The reformers have gone into hiding. Dictatorship is coming," he said.[2] Shevardnadze blamed what he called "reactionary forces"—conservative opponents of Gorbachev's policies—for trying to destroy *perestroika* and for driving him from office. His dramatic act and grim words stunned the Soviet Union and the world. They also highlighted the enormous obstacles blocking further democratic reform in the Soviet Union.

PRELUDE TO THE COUP

As 1990 ended, the Soviet Union and Mikhail Gorbachev reached an impasse. Between 1985 and 1990 tremendous progress had been made in reforming the country. The Soviet Union had held free elections and planted the seeds for genuinely democratic political institutions. The print and broadcast media had taken some giant steps along the long road from being a controlled government mouthpiece to becoming a free press. Between five and six million people had legally broken from the state-controlled economy and established independent cooperatives and private businesses. Workers had won the right to form independent trade unions and to strike. And the Soviet Union, like the United States, Europe, and the rest of the world, had finally been freed from the crippling expense and terrifying danger of the Cold War.

The problem was that along with the progress came great turbulence, disorder, and pain. The Soviet economy was in a shambles, and millions were suffering as a result. Ethnic tensions threatened to tear the country apart. Political divisions, not just between conservatives and reformers, but between the reformers themselves, further undermined stability. Worried about increased opposition from powerful conservative forces in the Communist party, the military, the secret police, and other entrenched forces, Gorbachev hesitated to implement additional reforms. As 1990 ended and 1991 began, he began to rely on the conservative forces that had opposed his recent radical reforms to now help him restore order. It is likely that Shevardnadze's resignation was intended to push Gorbachev back onto the path of reform.

If that was Shevardnadze's aim, he did not succeed. The conservative reaction quickened during the early months of 1991. On Sunday, January 13, Soviet troops armed with tanks and machine guns stormed the main radio and television station in Vilnius, the capital of Lithuania. More than a dozen people were killed and close to 200 were injured during the assault. A week later, a similar though smaller incident in Latvia, just to the north of Lithuania, cost four lives. The month of January also saw the appointment of a new prime minister who was clearly identified with conservative party elements, the introduction of army patrols to reinforce local police in several cities, and Gorbachev's call for suspension of a new law which had guaranteed freedom of the press. In February, several independent-minded television public affairs programs were cancelled, and news broadcasts began delivering only the government's version of events.

During March President Gorbachev once again tried to rally the country to his side. The Soviet Union had its first-ever nationwide referendum. The question at issue was direct and to-the-point: should the Soviet Union continue to exist as a unified country? Gorbachev staked his prestige on a positive answer, and in fact over three-quarters of those voting supported the president. However, six non-Russian republics, including the three Baltic republics, boycotted the election. What's more, in some areas other questions that Gorbachev opposed were added to the ballot, including one calling for direct election of the president of the Russian republic, the largest of the Soviet Union's fifteen republics. That question was strongly supported by Boris Yeltsin, whose growing popularity had turned him into Gorbachev's main rival. Yeltsin's ballot question passed overwhelmingly.

The next several months followed a familiar pattern: Gorbachev enjoyed success abroad and experienced failure at home. In July, he and President Bush signed a major arms control agreement in Moscow to cut long-range nuclear missiles by one-third. However, at home the economy and public order continued to deteriorate. Early in August, Alexander Yakovlev, the intellectual godfather of *perestroika*, resigned from the Communist party, thereby cutting his last ties to Gorbachev. As was true of Shevardnadze before him, Yakovlev warned of the dangers of a conservative coup against Gorbachev. Meanwhile, many public opinion polls showed that Gorbachev's popularity was continuing to fall in tandem with the decline of the Soviet economy. Despite the turmoil swirling around him, on August 4 Gorbachev departed for the Crimea in the southern part of the Soviet Union for a well-deserved vacation.

Gorbachev was scheduled to return by August 20, when most of the Soviet Union's fifteen republics were expected to sign a treaty that would redesign the country. The new Union Treaty, as it was called, would have allowed each republic a far greater degree of independence than before. However, conservative forces bitterly opposed the treaty, and before it could be signed they struck directly at Gorbachev in a desperate attempt to prevent its adoption.

THE COUP OF AUGUST 19, 1991

On the morning of August 19, 1991, the world awoke to the shocking news that Mikhail Gorbachev had been removed from office. In an announcement that no one quite believed at the time, the people of the Soviet Union and the world were told that President Gorbachev had resigned his office "for health reasons." Conservative party leaders opposed to further reforms announced they were in control of the country.

With Gorbachev under house arrest in the Crimea, people everywhere waited anxiously for what would happen next. Would the Russian people, as they had so often done in the past, simply accept what leaders in the Kremlin had decreed? Millions of them, the overwhelming majority of the population, stayed on the sidelines and waited. But hundreds of thousands did not. Furious and desperate to preserve their hard-won gains, they poured into the streets of Moscow and Leningrad in defiance of the gray and grim Communist politicians who were trying to turn back the clock. Leadership of the

Soviet Union's reformers fell to President Boris Yeltsin, who barely two months earlier had become the first freely elected president of the Russian republic. Yeltsin for several years had been criticizing Gorbachev for going too slowly in his reforms. Now he rushed headlong to the support of his rival and fellow reformer.

On the first morning of the coup, in the center of Moscow, Yeltsin dramatically climbed on top of a tank whose crew had defected to the side of the reformers. From that steely perch he called on the people of the Soviet Union to resist the coup. Meanwhile, thousands of Yeltsin's supporters surrounded his headquarters, determined to defend him from troops loyal to the coup leaders. In Leningrad, the resistance was led by Anatoly Sobchak, the city's reformist mayor.

Faced by mass resistance from their countrymen, the army hesitated. Individual tanks, paratroopers, and entire army units defected to the resistance. One column of armored vehicles was stopped on the streets of Moscow by a crowd that shoved flowers into the barrels of its guns. Coal miners across the country went on strike against the coup. Leaders in several of the Soviet republics also joined the resistance movement. Support for Yeltsin and Gorbachev also came from abroad, most importantly from President George Bush.

Within three days, the coup had run its course. A pale and shaken Mikhail Gorbachev returned to Moscow, once again the president of the Soviet Union. But what would that union look like, and would it even survive, were questions that remained unanswered.

AFTERMATH AND EPILOGUE

Before the August coup, the Communist system in the Soviet Union had been dying a slow death. The failure of the coup was the blow that killed Soviet communism once and for all. A wholesale dismantling of Communist institutions began. One of the first steps was also the most important: the Communist party was suspended in most parts of the country. Gorbachev himself resigned as its general secretary. The party's property was seized, and officials were forbidden to operate inside key institutions such as the KGB, the army, and the police. Its activities in factories, where dreary party meetings had long been a way of life, also were banned.

The top leaders in the KGB and the army were dismissed, and many of them were arrested. The army faced a drastic cut in its budget and the loss of most of its top officers. A reformer was put in charge of the feared KGB. His job was to pare the organization down to size and sever its ties to the army and the party. The organization that had been the "sword and shield" of the Communist party would be turned into one that would be suited to serve a democratic regime, not a dictatorship.

Central ministries of the government were closed down and many of their functions were transferred to the republics. The Komsomol, the party's youth organization that had trained its future leaders, dissolved itself. Meanwhile, the renaming of cities and towns began. Sverdlovsk, the city in which Tsar Nicholas II and his family were murdered, returned to its prerevolutionary name of Ekateringrad. More important and symbolic of the utter collapse of the old system, Leningrad once again became St. Petersburg, the name its founder Tsar Peter the Great gave it in 1703.

Perhaps most symbolic of all, on November 7, 1991, there were no official celebrations of the Bolshevik Revolution. Instead, in the recently renamed St. Petersburg, a man born in 1917, the year of the revolution, was visiting Russia for the first time. He was the Grand Duke Vladimir Kirillovich Romanov, who as the grandnephew of the murdered Tsar Nicholas II, was first in line for the nonexistent Russian throne. The Grand Duke's visit was a private one, with no official political meaning.

As communism collapsed inside the Soviet Union, the union itself began to crumble. Within two weeks of the coup, the struggle between the Baltic states of Lithuania, Latvia, and Estonia and the Soviet central government ended. On September 6, 1991, the Soviet government recognized the independence of all three nations, fifty-one years after they had been occupied by Stalin's soldiers. Gorbachev then began a last ditch attempt to hold the Soviet Union together, but he faced powerful forces that already were far beyond his control. On December 1 the people of the Ukraine voted in a referendum overwhelmingly for independence. A week later Boris Yeltsin and the leaders of Ukraine and Belorussia banged the last nails into the Soviet Union's coffin. They announced the formation of what they called the Commonwealth of Independent States, which would replace the Soviet Union. Yeltsin and his partners said the new commonwealth would be a loose union of sovereign states cooperating on problems such as mutual defense and economic issues while each state maintained its independence. Less than two weeks later, the commonwealth of independent states was formally constituted by eleven of the former Soviet republics. Only Latvia, Estonia, Lithuania, and Georgia remained outside the new commonwealth.

On December 25, Mikhail Gorbachev, a president without a country to govern, resigned as president of the nonexistent Soviet Union. At the conclusion of his speech the red soviet flag with its hammer and sickle, the symbol of Soviet communism, was lowered from over the Kremlin for the last time. It was replaced by the white, blue, and red flag of the newly independent Russian republic. The Union of Soviet Socialist Republics, the world's first socialist state and once mighty superpower, was no more.

The collapse of the Soviet Union left a huge power vacuum in the heart of the Eurasian land mass. It also left enormously important unanswered questions, for nobody knew if the Commonwealth of Independent States could prevent chaos from engulfing this vast region. It was impossible to tell what shape the commonwealth would take or if it would survive at all. Back in 1917, when the Russian empire collapsed, there was great optimism that it would be replaced by something better. As 1992 dawned, the Soviet Union's seventy-four-year history made it tragically clear that those hopeful expectations had been misplaced. As one often-heard saying went, the Soviet experience had been "seventy years on the road to nowhere." The wreckage of the Soviet Union floated into history to join the old Russian empire, and those who had endured continued to hope that this time, finally, their dreams of a better life would be fulfilled.

SOURCE
NOTES

CHAPTER 5: GORBACHEV AND *PERESTROIKA*

1   Martin Walker. *The Waking Giant* (New York: Pantheon, 1986), 245.

CHAPTER 6: THE HEIGHT OF *PERESTROIKA*

1   *Pravda*, August 2, 1986.

2   *The New York Times*, July 2, 1988, A1.

3   *The New York Times*, May 31, 1989, A6.

CHAPTER 7: THE FORMER SOVIET UNION IN THE NEW DECADE

1   Gabriel Schoenfeld, "Red Storm Rising," *The Atlantic Monthly*, December 1990.

2   *The New York Times*, December 21, 1990, A1.

GLOSSARY

Absolute dictator: A ruler with complete control over a country, who maintains that control through oppression and force.

Autocracy: A government where all power and authority is concentrated in a single person; a term used to describe the Russian government under the tsars.

Capitalism: An economic system characterized by a free market in which most economic activity is driven by the desire to gain a profit. Modern capitalism developed in Europe sometime after 1500 and eventually gave rise to the Industrial Revolution.

Cold War: The forty-five-year era of rivalry and tension between the Soviet Union and the democratic nations of the West, which was led by the United States, began after World War II and lasted until 1990. It was marked by the most expensive arms race in history, and in particular by a massive buildup of nuclear weapons.

Collectivization: The Soviet policy of forcing peasants to give up their private farms and work on large farms that supposedly were cooperatives but in reality were controlled by the Communist party. Collectivization was carried out in the late 1920s and early 1930s with great violence and led to the death of millions of peasants.

Counterculture: Most often refers to the life-style of young people in their teens and twenties who reject many of the values of their society. The term was used in reference to young people in the United States in the 1960s and 1970s, and later was applied to a variety of trends among Soviet youths, especially beginning in the 1980s.

Dekulakization: The policy of forcing the Soviet Union's more prosperous peasants off the land during collectivization. Millions of people were either driven into exile to remote areas of the Soviet Union or sent to labor camps where many died. Dekulakization resulted in the loss of millions of lives.

Gallows: A device used to execute people by hanging.

Industrialization: The building of modern industry. Industrialization took place in Western Europe and the United States in the late eighteenth and nineteenth centuries. Russia lagged behind the West in this important economic development.

Kulaks: The more prosperous peasants in Russia. Often resented by poorer neighbors, the class was destroyed by Stalin during collectivization.

Liberals: In prerevolutionary Russia, liberals were people who wanted their country to move gradually toward political democracy and capitalism.

Mir: The peasant commune in prerevolutionary Russia. It featured a form of self-government and performed important functions, such as collecting taxes and redistributing farmland among its member households. As a collector of taxes and in several other tasks, it functioned in effect as an agent of the tsarist government. The mir existed under serfdom and was retained when the serfs were emancipated, thereby limiting the freedom of Russia's peasants even though serfdom had been abolished.

Nationalists: People who are devoted to promoting the interests of their country.

Populists: Russians who believed that Russia's peasants were by nature socialists and that therefore Russia could build socialism without first going through capitalism. Populism was the dominant form of socialism among Russia's intelligentsia during the mid-nineteenth century. Later it was challenged by Marxism.

Proletariat: A Marxist term that refers to the working class in modern factories under capitalism. According to Marxism, the proletariat would be the class that would make the socialist revolution.

Satellite: In political terms, a country that while formally independent really is under the control of a more powerful country. Refers most often to the states in Eastern Europe that were under Soviet control from the end of World War II until 1989.

Serfdom: A condition in which peasant farmers are tied to the land and under the control of landlords, for whom they must perform a specified amount of work. Serfs in Western Europe during the Middle Ages had certain, if limited, rights, and therefore were quite different from slaves. Serfs in Russia had fewer rights than European serfs, and their status therefore often was similar to that of slaves.

Socialists: People who believe in an economic system based on the public ownership of a society's wealth rather than on private property, and on cooperation rather than competition as the most efficient and fairest way to order economic activity.

Soviet: Means "council" in Russian. During both 1905 and 1917 Russian working people and soldiers formed soviets to represent their interests, and these organizations played an important role in revolutions. The most famous and important soviets were the St. Petersburg Soviet (1905) and the Petrograd Soviet (1917). After 1917 the term referred to organs of the Communist government which had no independence and were controlled by the Communist party.

Steppe: A grassland or prairie. Most often refers to the great prairie of southern Russia.

Taiga: Usually describes the huge forest belt stretching across the northern part of Russia from its western borders to the Pacific Ocean. The term can refer to similar forest regions elsewhere in the world.

Totalitarian society: A society in which the government exercises extraordinary control over its citizens, not permitting any independent institutions to exist. Totalitarianism is more extreme than the old Russian autocracy because it makes use of twentieth-century technology and plays a more active role in determining what its people do. Stalinist Russia was one of the most extreme of the totalitarian societies of this century.

Tundra: An arctic area south of the polar ice cap with a permanently frozen subsoil. Vegetation consists of lichens, mosses, and a few shrubs.

Veches: Russian town assemblies during the Kievan era, although some survived a while longer. Most were destroyed during the Mongol era, and the few survivors were eliminated as the power of the Russian autocracy grew in the fourteenth and fifteenth centuries.

FOR FURTHER READING

Aganbegyan, Abel, ed. *Perestroika 1989*. New York: Charles Scribner's Sons, 1988.

Daniels, Robert V. *Is Russia Reformable?* Boulder, Colo., and London: Westview Press, 1988.

Davies, R. W. *Soviet History in the Gorbachev Revolution*. Bloomington and Indianapolis: Indiana University Press, 1989.

Desai, Padma. *Perestroika in Perspective*. Princeton, N.J.: Princeton University Press, 1989.

Eklof, Ben. *Soviet Briefing*. Boulder, Colo., and London: Westview Press, 1989.

Goldman, Marshall L. *Gorbachev's Challenge: Economic Reform in the Age of High Technology*. New York and London: Norton, 1987.

Hough, Jerry. *Russia and the West: Gorbachev and the*

Politics of Reform. New York: Simon and Schuster, 1988.

Kerblay, Basile. *Gorbachev's Russia*. New York: Pantheon, 1989.

Kort, Michael. *The Soviet Colossus: A History of the USSR*, 2d ed. Boston and London: Unwin Hyman, 1990.

Lewin, Moshe. *The Gorbachev Phenomenon*. Berkeley and Los Angeles: University of California Press, 1989.

Oberg, James E. *Uncovering Soviet Disasters: Exploring the Limits of Glasnost*. New York: Random House, 1988.

Rywkin, Michael. *Soviet Society Today*. New York: M. E. Sharpe, 1989.

Tarasulo, Isaac J., ed. *Gorbachev and Glasnost: Viewpoints from the Soviet Press*. Wilmington, Del.: Scholarly Resources, 1989.

Taubman, William, and Jane Taubman. *Moscow Spring*. New York: Summit Books, 1989.

INDEX

Russia (*cont.*)
nineteenth-century
reforms, 24–26
revolutionary movement,
27–29
Russian autocracy, 18–19
Russian Orthodox Church, 86
Russian Republic, 106
Rybakov, Anatoly, 84
Ryzhkov, Nikolai, 71, 106

Sakharov, Andrei, 59, 84, 87,
90–91
Secret police, 37, 41, 45–46,
51, 66, 92, 109
Serfdom, 20–21, 24–25
Shcharansky, Anatoly, 83–84
Shevardnadze, Eduard, 71,
106, 110, 111
Sobchak, Anatoly, 106, 114
Social problems, 59, 64,
98–100
Solzhenitsyn, Alexander, 54,
59, 84–85
Soviet Union, 5, 7–9
under Andropov, 59
under Brezhnev, 56–59
under Chernenko, 59–60
collapse of, 101–117
under Gorbachev, 61–77,
78–100
under Khrushchev, 50–56
land, 9–12
under Lenin, 36–40
people, 12–13
under Stalin, 41–49

Sputnik I, Soviet satellite, 54
Stalin, Joseph, 9, 36, 38, 40,
41–49, 80, 86. *See also*
Destalinization process
Stravinsky, Igor, 26

Tchaikovsky, Peter, 26
Tolstoy, Leo, 26
Totalitarianism, 46–47
Treaty of Brest-Litovsk, 36–37
Trotsky, Leon, 36, 38, 41, 42

Ukraine, 96, 108, 116
United States, 49, 54, 58, 68,
72, 87

Vladimir, Kievan prince, 16
Voznesensky, Andrei, 75

World War I, 31, 33, 34, 35,
36–37
World War II, 47–49

Yakovlev, Alexander, 82, 106,
112
Yazov, Dmitri, 82
Yeltsin, Boris, 82–83, 91,
106, 114, 116
Yevtushenko, Yevgeny, 69–70
Youth underground culture,
98–100
Yugoslavia, 49

Zamiatin, Yevgeny, 83

DATE DUE			
JUL 29 '94			
MAR 11 95			
APR 12 95			
APR 18 96			
MAR 31 97			
MAY 8 '97			